# *Breakthroughs*

RE-CREATING THE AMERICAN CITY

# *Breakthroughs*

## RE-CREATING THE AMERICAN CITY

**NEAL R. PEIRCE**
**and**
**ROBERT GUSKIND**

CENTER FOR URBAN POLICY RESEARCH

Published by the Center for Urban Policy Research
Rutgers, the State University of New Jersey
Livingston Campus—Building 4161
New Brunswick, New Jersey 08903



Printed in the United States of America

Book design by Helene Berinsky

*Library of Congress Cataloging in Publication Data*

Peirce, Neal R.
Breakthroughs : re-creating the American city / Neal R. Peirce and Robert Guskind.
p. cm.
Includes index.
ISBN 0-88285-145-4 : $24.95
1. City planning—United States—History—20th century—Case studies. 2. Urban renewal—United States—Case studies. 3. Central business districts—United States—Case studies. I. Guskind, Robert. II. Title
NA9105.P45 1993
307.1'216'0973—dc20 93–17189
CIP

## *CONTENTS*

# *FOREWORD*

Lewis Mumford, the American writer and social scientist, wrote that cities were created as "a means of bringing heaven down to earth." They are a "symbol of the possible." His idealism is hard to grasp these days when our cities have become symbols of despair. Solving urban problems sometimes seems impossible.

At the Bruner Foundation in Manhattan, we remain hopeful. Time and again, we have watched people do the impossible: transform their neighborhoods, cities, and even regions through innovative, collective action.

These successful models of urban excellence should be celebrated, and their success must be examined so that their lessons can be applied across the nation. The Rudy Bruner Award for Excellence in the Urban Environment was founded in 1986 to help make this happen. Primarily, the award is a tool of discovery. Searching for worthy programs, we attempt to find out what kinds of things improve cities. With the urban crisis growing and resources shrinking, false solutions must be avoided; the cost in human terms is too high.

It is the rigorous, innovative process by which the Bruner Foundation evaluates urban places that lends the award special value. Each round of competition takes two years. The Selection Committee members are chosen not only for their reputation in particular areas of expertise, such as landscape architecture or community development, but for displaying receptivity to issues outside their respective fields.

Over the years, Bruner selection committees have tried to avoid defining urban excellence too narrowly. A simplistic perspective is one reason so many urban projects—even projects that win architecture or design awards—sometimes bring disappointing results in both human and economic terms.

We believe the development process to be a highly complex contest involving diverse perspectives and goals, none of which is sufficient in itself to create excellent urban places: developers and architects pursue economic and aesthetic objectives; governments promote their planning and growth policies; and neighborhood groups focus on the quality of life in their communities.

The Rudy Bruner Award competition seeks to identify, reward, and publicize urban places that reconcile these competing objectives. The economic, visual, and social perspectives must complement one another.

Although the limits that define eligible submissions for the award are quite broad, the project must be a real place, not just a plan. It must demonstrate its excellence in action. The people affected by the project must be involved. The values should be explicit and viewed as worthwhile by the local community. Conflicts must be discussed and resolved openly. Besides showing social responsibility, economic viability, and aesthetic sensitivity, the projects must also be ecologically benign.

With this broad mandate as a backdrop, each Bruner Award Selection Committee walks onto an empty stage without a script. The debate about what constitutes urban excellence begins afresh with each round of competition, inspired and framed by the eighty to ninety detailed responses to our call for submissions.

The senior author of *Breakthroughs: Re-Creating the American City,* Neal R. Peirce, is one of America's most knowledgeable urban journalists who served as a Rudy Bruner Award Selection Committee member and who participated vigorously in the debate that designated New York City's Tenant Interim Lease Program and Portland's Downtown Plan and Program as 1989 winners.

At the end of each chapter, critical conversations have been included in order to provide additional perspectives on the projects described. The contributors to these commentaries include Robert Shibley and Polly Welch, longtime consultants to the Bruner Foundation, as well as members of the Selection Committee who evaluated the award entries: Mary Decker, director of Capital Planning and Policy, Board of Commissioners of Cook County, Illinois; George E. Hartman, Jr., a partner in the Washington, D.C., architectural firm of Hartman-Cox; David Lawrence, senior vice president of Gerald Hines Interests, a Houston-based real estate firm; Steve Livingston, director of the Department of Parks, Charleston, South Carolina; the Honorable Joseph P. Riley, Jr., mayor of Charleston; Anne Whiston Spirn, professor of landscape architecture and regional planning at the University of Pennsylvania in Philadelphia; and Aaron Zaretsky, the former executive director of the Market Foundation in Seattle and currently the executive director of the Grove Arcade Public Market Foundation in Ashville, North Carolina. Robert Shibley is the director of urban design and a professor of planning and architecture in the School of Architecture and Planning at the State University of New York at Albany. Polly Welch, an architect, is the former deputy assistant secretary of public housing in the Executive Office of Communities and Development of the commonwealth of Massachusetts.

Simeon Bruner
Treasurer, Board of Trustees
Bruner Foundation

# INTRODUCTION

It has never been easy for American cities. They have been obliged to survive in a nation born into Jeffersonian agrarianism and later to mature into suburban flight. Large or small, America's cities have had a perennially difficult time generating admiration, respect, or understanding. They have served the nation magnificently as fountainheads of commerce, finance, and the arts. They have taken millions of new Americans from their point of entry and helped those newcomers elevate themselves economically into the American mainstream. In recent years, the greatest of cities—such as New York, Chicago, and Los Angeles—have become command centers of a new global economy.

Yet in the popular American image, the cities have rarely come off well despite the fact that it was to the cities that masses of immigrants and racial minorities first came, to those cities that generated the most social tensions and that harbored the most notorious political machines. Organized crime, drug rings, and frightening crime rates all acquired a distinctly urban aura, and from generation to generation, rural and then suburban politicians found cities their safest whipping boy.

The problems of American cities go deeper than image, or the fact that they have lost much of their backbone of solid income-earning residents, or the reality that the vast majority of the menial and manufacturing jobs they could once offer strong-backed but ill-educated newcomers has disappeared in the years since World War II. With their loss of the middle class and with the waning of self-confident, homegrown business leadership and strong ethnic neighborhoods in the era following World War II, cities have become tougher places to lead, to coalesce for the common good. Cities and their citizens feel acted upon, victims of vast demographic, economic, and social forces far beyond their control. Ordinary residents often feel they are more victims than beneficiaries of massive urban bureaucracies whose chief interest seems to be protecting their own institutional prerogatives.

Sometimes it seems as if *nothing* civic, of general benefit, can be achieved in American cities. Out in the neighborhoods, the so-called NIMBY syndrome—"not in my backyard"—surfaces to block halfway houses, havens for the homeless, even hiding places for battered women. Residents who toil to save their homes, to turn around deteriorating communities, sometimes receive a not-so-subtle message, even from their own city's leaders, that it might be easier to pack up and leave than to stay and fight, that entire neighborhoods are doomed to failure. An architect proposes a truly creative new building or public space and investors begin to carp that it is too expensive, that corners had better be cut. Business or citizen reformers, trying to reinvigorate school systems that do not teach or to shake up police forces that cannot stop crime, get shunted aside by unions and entrenched, civil service–protected staffs.

This book is not principally about these problems of urban life, however real they are. This is a book, rather, about the glowing exceptions, the *breakthroughs,* the tentative, fragile, critical lead indicators that might lead to stronger urban societies in the twenty-first century. It is a chronicle—a sampler, if you will—of six efforts selected because of their exemplary approach to urban problem solving by the Rudy Bruner Award. Each of them, in deeply individual ways, offers nuggets of hope and guidance to American policymakers seeking to recover from the excesses and failures of the 1960s-style Great Society social tinkering and the callous neglect and denial of the minimalist policies of the Reagan era.

When one looks across today's American cityscape, there *are* exceptions to urban mediocrity, discouragement, and complacency: collaborative city planning efforts that can, and do, work; housing programs that can function without being throttled by bureaucracy; local governments that bend themselves into new shapes and forms to accommodate their citizens; a revived city market or new urban plaza that is a joy to walk through; schools that ignite a love of learning, of possibility, in their students; police systems that treat citizens more as allies than suspects; community-based partnerships that create new housing and new enterprises even when government agencies claim it cannot be done.

Out of the ferment of the 1980s, and perhaps out of the desperation it created, a new urban theory is taking shape. It can be found in seemingly disparate elements—people, public-private partnerships, at first glance off-the-wall coalitions—that somehow coalesce to forge new approaches to old problems and new dilemmas alike.

No single definition of urban success springs out among the diverse models for nurturing and re-creating a new, more viable, and, yes, more human city. For some, it may be building a neighborhood with a genuine sense of community, a place with an internal support system that functions family to family, neighbor to neighbor, the kind of neighborhood that many of us can remember as a vibrant, caring place. A *community.* Others see it in a school system or a police force that responds to the needs of the people it should serve and is, in fact, in large measure controlled by them. Others think the great city is one with "good" urban design, though there is great debate about what that is: Is it a "signature building" that makes the pages of major architectural reviews? A plaza that buzzes with activity in broad daylight and after dark? A park that invites users from diverse neighborhoods to mix on common ground? Perhaps, even more broadly, the right mix of design and social sensitivity that leads to appealing *public* spaces, whether a broad downtown plaza or a pocket neighborhood park?

The truth, of course, is that urban success, the urban genius starting to bud across our cities, can be defined by any of these elements, and more. Positive urban breakthroughs rest not so much on electing brilliant people to office—though it is surely handy to have them there—as on the birth of a civic culture of cooperation and a belief in the future, with individuals willing to take up the torch to make that better future a reality. The rebirth process hinges on developing and cultivating a sense of the possible, even in the face of the seemingly formidable odds that confront every urban resident, whether he or she lives in Boston, New York City, Atlanta, Houston, Milwaukee, or Denver.

Partnerships are a critical ingredient of the new approach. In the past, governments, corporations, churches, foundations, and nonprofit organizations all worked independently to fight poverty. Their efforts were well-intentioned but far too disjointed to make any impact. In the 1980s, in communities from Baltimore to Miami to Cleveland, these players learned how to work together to rebuild hard-pressed areas. Community groups—often community development corporations actually rehabilitating housing and starting new businesses—became involved in a broad set of partnerships with local governments, states, foundations, banks, and businesses. These alliances became the troubled neighborhoods' chief road to survival and growth in the 1980s as federal support for communities atrophied. Some new, extraordinarily significant intersocietal connections were made. They promise to become even more critical in the 1990s.

Thoughtful people have begun to recognize that the challenges in American society are far more complex than simply putting roofs over people's heads. They have to do with community. They have to do with assuring all Americans a safe place to live. Communities overrun by drugs, crime, and splintered families are not safe. Neither government housing authorities nor police rushing in with sirens wailing and lights flashing is capable of making them secure and decent. The most critical ingredient of neighborhood safety is neighbors insisting on safety in their own home turf. Neighbors know how to set standards and with peer pressure get them enforced. In order to work, revitalization efforts must address the intimate ties between housing, employment, education, and home conditions.

Indeed, traveling around America in the 1980s and early 1990s, there was a profound contrast between neighborhoods with a sense of their own identity and worth, and some measure of self-control, as opposed to those that simply received largess from government bureaucracies. With rare exceptions, for example, the low-income housing owned and administered by grass-roots organizations was superbly maintained. The contrast could not be more dramatic with the stereotypical run-down, graffiti-smeared, publicly run inner-city public housing development. Why? Again, because a neighborhood knows how to establish its own rules, its own order, and its own discipline in a way outsiders rarely if ever can.

The empowerment of people serves double duty. It is *the* critical vehicle for change, and it should be the overriding goal of any and all efforts to rebuild a city block, a neighborhood, or an entire community. Empowerment is perhaps one of the toughest changes policymakers will have to contend with in the 1990s, for it is far more easily proclaimed—made a political slogan—than achieved. The empowerment of people to improve their own lives has never been a clear-cut, executable strategy some high level of government can snap its fingers and effect. Just as racial divisions continue to plague our society and we have no simple formulas to reduce them, empowerment is a change that may be encouraged but basically must percolate upward. Faced with such dilemmas, public administration theory falters.

The new urban theory recognizes a communitywide "ecosystem" that, when it can be put in place, nurtures and enhances community-based development. There are important ingredients: committed civic leadership, an aggressive and competent state or city government, strong intermediary groups, a cast of supporting banks and insurance companies, foundations, and private corporations—plus people and a growing base of neighborhood leaders.

The new urban theory of our time is first and foremost about people—individuals who effect change in ways both small and grand; people who organize their communities against seemingly impossible odds; nonprofessionals who tackle problems that have stymied the so-called "pros" for years and manage to find some light at the end of the tunnel, even if they do not find *the* solution.

In the late 1980s, when the Ford Foundation set out to recognize the most innovative programs in state and local government around the nation, receiving literally thousands of entries, it discovered a most interesting phenomenon: Roughly half the programs singled out for special recognition were not conceived within the government at all; rather, they had originated with citizen activists who sold authorities on the idea and were then invited in to run the programs. Alternately, the fresh ideas originated somewhere far out in the tentacles of the bureaucracy, far from central headquarters, out of the day-to-day experience of government service providers. Then, instead of being quashed—the fate of many fresh ideas in large organizations—they were embraced by exceptionally farsighted administrators and carefully "sold" to the entire organization. In the overwhelmingly male world of local officialdom, many of the winning programs were run by, if not first proposed by, women. Even more was afoot than citizen activists and women making a strong mark: A handful of government administrators was finding ways to encourage innovative ideas from "down in the ranks" and making it clear they could tolerate failure in trial-and-error efforts in the hope of making large bureaucracies more responsive to the needs of ordinary people, their "customers." One got the idea that an avant-garde of progressive state and local government agencies is moving rapidly into the new age of participatory, nonhierarchical (or "bottoms-up") management already celebrated in such books as *In Search of Excellence: Lessons from America's Best Run Companies* (Warner Books, 1988).

In most places, practice lags leagues behind the best new theory. No clean-cut, simple solutions can be laid out for practitioners to duplicate. The urban theory that runs through the experiments described in this book tends to turn the very foundation of our centralized society upon its head and present, by contrast, a new world of quite unconventional approaches. In some cases, we even see sweeping, radical decentralization in which ordinary people, operating block by block, neighborhood by neighborhood, seize control of their own destiny and sometimes accomplish more in six months or a year than traditional governmental entities have managed to do in a decade of bitter fighting and flailing.

The six stories we relate in *Breakthroughs: Re-Creating the American City* are a seemingly disparate bunch—the tale of a grassroots housing program in New York City's toughest neighborhoods, for instance, or the saga of stopping a highway in Lincoln, Nebraska, and the struggle to undo several *decades* of governmental neglect and bungling.

The stories told here are not a clean cross section of the most promising experimentation in our cities, yet among the six projects profiled in these pages—projects singled out by the Rudy Bruner Award for their excellence in the urban environment—are the nuggets of new and powerful notions about urbanism one has to believe bear immense promise as the nation struggles to keep up with the new developments and challenges of the 1990s. They are stories about places and policy, tales about government and communities. Above all, they are stories about people: People who fight, at untold personal sacrifice, and win; men and women who serve as inspirations for entire neighborhoods; individuals who stand as counterweights to despair.

These are the six projects. Four are from cities. Two are actually out of rural America. All of them illustrate the vital import of individuals as catalysts:

- New York City's intriguing "TIL" (tenant interim lease) program, a landmark housing program that has enabled thousands of America's poorest minority people to become owners of their own apartments.
- The Portland Downtown Plan of 1972, credited for transforming the city's Willamette riverfront from a roaring traffic artery to a park, leading to a handsome bus mall and successful new light rail system, swimming against the tide to increase the downtown's share of regional retailing. The plan has helped make Portland, Oregon, one of the continent's liveliest, most appealing cities.
- Boston's Southwest Corridor, the story of how a fight against freeways culminated in a mass-transit line and neighborhood-sensitive development along its every mile. The project became the biggest public capital effort in Massachusetts history and is landmark testimony to how "officialdom" and citizens, poor and rich, can work together.
- Lincoln's "Radial Reuse" project, a lesson in how citizens can correct a monumental blunder by city hall and remake—for people and homes and community—a four-mile corridor that had been devastated to become a road corridor. In Lincoln, Nebraska, grass-

roots protest was transformed into rebuilding and a powerful lesson into learning how to think and act anew.

• Cabrillo Village, a California community rebuilt by farm workers who decided to take their future into their own hands and who organized to save their own homes. They ended up building new housing, providing vivid evidence that low-income housing can be aesthetically appealing and can reflect a village's strong native culture.

• Vermont's Stowe Recreation Path, at first glance simply a pedestrian and bicyclist way through a famed vacation resort town, but watch how the path operates and you discover a new place that every age group, every class of citizen enjoys as a new common ground, a Main Street for the automobile age, a model potentially as promising for great cities as small towns.

It is interesting that of these six finalists, the New York City TIL program and Portland's Downtown Plan—entries spanning a continent and worlds apart in their ostensible approach—eventually tied for the Rudy Bruner Award and received it jointly. The jury's dilemma, in retrospect, was predictable. The TIL program addresses, directly, America's problems of housing, social deprivation, and the nation's threatened polarized two-class society. By teaching existing tenants how to run and operate their buildings, it leads them toward the American dream of home ownership. The story is made all the more exciting by the fact that TIL buildings are located in some of America's meanest urban environments.

Yet the jury found Portland's 1972 Downtown Plan, and its follow-up over the years, equally exciting. The net result was no less than turning downtown Portland into one of America's most vibrant urban centers, making the downtown *work* in the age of the automobile and the surburban subdivision, when so many center cities have failed. In the process, albeit with travail, much low-income housing was preserved, an income mix was introduced into the downtown residential picture, historic preservation was honored, and magnificent public places were created. Immense technical and planning expertise, and the skill of great artists, went into the Portland plan, yet it worked principally because it never lost sight of its roots in the will of the people and it never lost its determination to improve every Portlander's quality of life.

## BONFIRES OF REALITY

The cynic may, of course, say: "It's nice to have highly original projects, but does the nation *need* a new theory of urban revival? Cities at least *look* better off than during the riots of the 1960s. As for the urban poor, they've been around since the dawn of time and we've done well anyway—especially here in America—so why don't we be realistic and accept more of the status quo?"

Our reply is: Tune on the evening news and watch the incredibly disturbing images that pass before us every day. In New York City, reality mirrored the fictional plot line of author Tom Wolfe's *The Bonfire of the Vanities* (Farrar, Straus & Giroux, 1987), the Big Apple yarn of materialism, class division, and poisonous racial tension. In a Queens neighborhood called Howard Beach, a gang of white thugs chased a black man—who had committed the sin of being in the wrong place at the wrong time—out onto a highway, where he was run down and killed. A young white professional woman was brutally attacked and gang raped in Central Park by black and Hispanic teenagers out for a night of "wilding" in an incident that became known as the case of the "Central Park jogger"—a national symbol for everything that has gone wrong in urban America. As if to confirm that everyone's fears were not terribly misplaced, a young man visiting New York City for the first time from Salt Lake City was stabbed to death trying to defend his parents from subway muggers who were out robbing for money so they could dance the Manhattan night away. The press, once again sounding a familiar refrain, began commiserating over the fate of the world's greatest city in glum terms that had not been heard in nearly two decades.

Boston. Chicago. Philadelphia. Atlanta. Miami. New Orleans. San Diego. No city has been immune from the daily onslaught of bad news that seemed to emanate from our urban centers. In such seemingly "safe" cities as Lincoln and Omaha, Nebraska, residents discovered that they were not safe from "big city" drug trafficking as the police moved in to shut down crackhouses doing a thriving business.

Los Angeles, America's Shangri-la on the West Coast, has begun to trade in an image as an oasis of palm trees, sunshine, and Hollywood for a grimmer reality of foul air, twenty-four-hour-a-day traffic jams, desperately poor immigrants, and drug-dealing gangs that traded blows in drive-by shootings. Sometimes it seemed that anytime one struck up a conversation with a Southern Californian, the topic would inevitably turn to the area's grave mismatch between jobs and homes, with remarks about how it might have taken him or her two hours to get to work from a home located sixty, seventy, even one hundred miles distant. The facts of life are chilling: the great majority of jobs are going into western Los Angeles and Orange counties and the bulk of remotely affordable new housing into Riverside and San Bernardino counties, many freeways away. The

L.A. 2000 citizen/business/civic committee, appointed by Mayor Tom Bradley, warned of a fearsome future:

> . . . a balkanized landscape of political fortresses, each guarding its own resources in the midst of divisiveness, overcrowded freeways, antiquated sewers, ineffective schools, inadequate human services and a polluted environment.

Old-fashioned political corruption reattacked the cities in the 1980s. In the nation's capital, a city government battered by corruption and ineptitude was shaken to the core when Mayor Marion Barry was videotaped by the FBI during a sting operation smoking crack in a hotel room. In Atlantic City, the East Coast's outpost of casino gambling and one of the nation's saddest cities, virtually the entire elected local government was indicted and hauled off to jail for corruption. In New York City, officials were picked off in droves in one of the most far-reaching, pervasive corruption scandals uncovered in the twentieth century. That such public malfeasance and inefficiency continued to thrive in an era when public money was in critically short supply made the imperative of intelligent management even more critical and the tragedy of the squandering of scarce resources even more poignant.

Meanwhile, nearly every city began to sag under the combined weight of federal cutbacks and skyrocketing demands for social services. The era of President Ronald W. Reagan and "scorched earth" federal domestic budgets had not been kind. Reagan's eagerness to cut federal assistance to the cities—a policy he proclaimed and the American public seemed to endorse in two landslide elections—had become virtually enshrined in a national budget with twelve-digit federal deficits stretching into the infinite future. All one had to do was examine any urban need, whether it was rotting bridges and potholed roads or miserable housing, and the outlook for federal assistance was the same: negligible. Before Reagan was elected president, federal aid amounted to 26 percent of what the nation's cities raised from their own tax sources. By 1988, it was down to 7.5 percent. For many cities, such reductions amounted to real losses in federal aid of upward of $200 million a year.

Fiscal prudence, of course, was often missing at city hall. In 1990, it seemed the nation might be in for a repeat of the 1970s when such cities as Cleveland and New York faced a dismal fiscal abyss. Philadelphia, the city where the Declaration of Independence and the U.S. Constitution were written, became the first major American city to succumb to the cresting urban financial nightmare. Strained to the breaking point by constricted tax revenues, loss of federal aid, and an indifferent state legislature, the city teetered perilously close to the edge of bankruptcy through much of 1990 and 1991. Similarly ominous rumblings were heard in Boston, New York City, San Francisco, and countless other cities.

City school systems performed so abysmally that a neighborhood-business alliance in Chicago got the state legislature to wrest control from the massive downtown school bureaucracy and vest it largely in popularly elected, parent-controlled school committees for each of the city's 590 schools. Across the nation, dropout rates approached and exceeded 50 percent in many of the largest cities. Teenage pregnancy continued at staggeringly high levels, with as many as one in every two births in the inner city coming to unwed young mothers. School governance was proving itself so inept that Boston and other cities talked of dismantling their school boards, shifting education to the control of general purpose government.

From Los Angeles to Chicago, Washington, D.C., to Atlanta, local prison systems were so full of criminals that there was no place left to warehouse them. Courts were so overwhelmed they generally were incapable of even processing the few offenders that hard-pressed law enforcement officials managed to catch and bring to justice. Everywhere urban hospitals were finding themselves coping with seemingly endless streams of patients—suffering from everything from the common cold to AIDS (acquired immune deficiency syndrome) and gunshot wounds—that taxed them to the breaking point. Chicago's hospital system, one of the nation's finest, had already come nightmarishly close to breaking down, overwhelmed by a wave of hospital closings and a frightening crush of emergency cases brought on by poor, inner-city patients with nowhere to turn.

On the social front, AIDS cut a devastating path through the homosexual community concentrated in urban areas, made frightening headway among heterosexuals in many minority communities, and threatened to create new financial and social burdens for cities that would haunt them through the 1990s and beyond.

The ranks of the homeless swelled to frightening proportions in the big city and small town alike. In New York City, thousands made their homes in bus terminals and train stations and panhandlers stationed themselves on virtually every street corner. In warmer climates, entire families lived in their cars or in crude Third World–style shantytowns underneath expressways or anywhere they could find a modicum of shelter. Desperate-looking men rummaged through the trash and combed magnificent Southern California beaches from San Diego to Los Angeles to Santa Barbara. Tattered men and women could be seen pushing shopping carts full of meager belongings on rural roads from northern Indiana to central Florida. At times, it seemed that American cities were in a perverse competition to see which could best approximate the place described by Charles Dickens in *A Tale of Two Cities.*

The late 1970s and 1980s brought the *best* news in a generation to urban America: People who had abandoned downtowns in the 1950s and 1960s rediscovered the unique joy of the city. During the 1980s, American downtowns, from Boston and Baltimore to Chicago and Minneapolis, experienced the biggest, most concentrated building booms of their history. Their skylines burgeoned and were transformed as a new generation of superbuildings—some commonplace, others quite intriguing in varieties of postmodernist garb—rose in downtowns across America. Architects such as Phillip Johnson and Helmut Jahn took their place on the American landscape side by side with Mies van der Rohe and Louis Sullivan, a new generation of urban designers for a new era of downtown building. Center cities once written off as dead found new life as attractions such as festival marketplaces, aquariums, convention centers, and other "magnets" began to attract both resident and visitor alike.

In Boston, developer James Rouse opened Faneuil Hall in 1976, a wildly successful festival market near Boston Harbor. Imitators swarmed to the scene. By the end of the 1980s, there was scarcely a major American city without a festival marketplace or new downtown shopping mall. Some were successful and helped touch off downtown revivals; others were far less so (and quite a few went bankrupt). Projects such as Rouse's Faneuil Hall and Harborplace in Baltimore were joyful and sensitively designed environments adding immeasurable vitality to the cityscape. Others tended to be walled-off enclaves turning their back on the urban fabric.

Architectural gems or bad jokes, they all stood as evidence of the rebirth of confidence in the American city. Even some of the nation's most hard-up cities, places such as Newark, New Jersey, so buffeted by adverse social tides that they embodied urban rot in the American consciousness, began to experience modest downtown building revivals. The resurrection of such cities was scarcely conceivably for anyone who had witnessed the glowing embers of 1967 and 1968 when one American center after another was racked by brutal and destructive riots.

Still, the hard questions remained: To what end? How far would the newfound life and prosperity of the American downtown spread? Would the struggling residents of New York City's Bedford-Stuyvesant, Boston's Roxbury, Newark's Central Ward, or Chicago's South Side share in the revival or would they become bystanders stranded on a periphery that became further removed from a miragelike prosperity they could see but could not touch?

As Robert Gannett, a Chicago neighborhood activist, told us in 1987, "We really fear a tale of two cities where we're left with a thriving lakefront while the rest of the city is devastated."

The same concern, the same observation could have been valid for virtually Any City USA. The American city, of course, had not quite become Rio de Janeiro, where the shantytowns of the desperately poor—*favelas* so wrought with crime and lawlessness that even the police feared entering many of them—hug mountainsides overlooking the homes and playgrounds of the mind-bogglingly wealthy. Still, as the gap between have and have-not widened, it was hard to ignore the kinds of urban contrasts that Americans assumed were relegated to the Third World. The nation appeared to be starting the 1990s in evermore polarized, isolated camps of race and income.

A successful lawyer could dine on formal china in a glitzy downtown restaurant while a beggar jangled a cup with change within his sight. The tenement dweller was entitled to a million-dollar view of awe-inspiring skylines out the window and filthy streets teaming with poverty and deprivation out the front door. Neighborhoods struggled for economic crumbs and city services while there seemed to be no end to the interest and investment in downtown. A young executive could finish off a day at work, stroll down to one of those new gourmet grocery stores that sold twenty-four different varieties of pâté and little vegetables produced more for show than for taste, then head off to the gym for a workout on a $20,000 piece of exercise equipment while entire neighborhoods and even cities remained bereft of basic grocery stores, banks, restaurants, and even movie theaters.

None of the contrasts were new. A check of New York City's history alone would reveal frightening past contrasts of immigrant working classes living in squalor while the wealthy luxuriated in comfort. Fires once ravaged great stretches of the urban landscape; street urchins starved or froze to death; poor women died in childbirth without medical attention; municipal thievery outmatched anything we have seen for a half century or more. A century ago, New York City's Lower East Side alone harbored some 1.5 million people, mostly immigrants, jammed into hovels and rat-infested buildings.

However, all that was before a careful social safety net had, ostensibly, been constructed to help a nation's less fortunate, before Social Security, Medicaid and Medicare, and innumerable new protections. As if a more developed social conscience were not good enough reason to be concerned, there was the reality that the United States was plunged into an increasingly tough global economic competition—and that its most advanced competitors, the Europeans and Japanese in particular, had far more sophisticated social support, child-care, educational, and school-to-work programs in place. That meant that their populations would be measurably more competent—that is, competitive—in the years ahead. American public costs, even for the most elementary social services, were sure to soar—not to mention expenditures for prisons, which were already skyrocketing. The bottom line was that urban waste of people was becoming a less and less affordable American "luxury."

By the late 1980s, Americans faced such jarring realities as nearly two-thirds of black children being born to unwed mothers. More than half of all black families were headed by women, and in some of the nation's cities, the figure approached 90 percent. Some 70 percent of the children in those families were growing up poor. A new generation of academicians found a career studying the "under class," the most desperately poor of all Americans—largely black in America's cities, white in rural areas, and women and children for the most part. Brilliantly chronicled by New York City writer Ken Auletta in *The Underclass* (Random House, 1982), they were Americans permanently stuck on a poverty treadmill: outcasts, drug dealers, hard-core unemployed, single mothers caught up in the welfare system, deranged vagrants and other homeless, illiterate teenagers, muggers, burglars, and murderers. They numbered between one million and more than ten million, depending on which academic was applying which set of standards in making the count. The emergence of the underclass through the 1970s and 1980s represented, in the words of William Julius Wilson, a University of Chicago sociologist, "one of the most important social transformations of the last quarter of the twentieth century."

Meanwhile, America was at work building a new generation of cities—the so-called "urban village"—great suburban and exurban concentrations of office buildings, shopping centers, and subdivisions that leapfrogged across the landscape in ever-widening circles away from the central cities and their problems. Bedroom communities became boardroom cities, home to every imaginable economic interest, from America's biggest corporate giants to its smallest upstate industries. Small country roads were transformed from meandering, scenic byways into roaring traffic arteries so underequipped to handle the strain that rush hours seemed to stretch from dawn until dusk with little letup in between.

The runaway suburban growth of the decade changed the nation's economic face and balance of power forever. The Office Network in Houston, a real estate group that kept track of such things, reported that in the 1970s, only 25 percent of America's office space was located in central cities. By the end of the 1980s, however, the balance had been dramatically, and perhaps irrevocably, altered. Some 60 percent of the nation's office space was now in far-flung urban villages, places with names like Tysons Corner, Virginia, or Southfield, Michigan, many of which did not even appear on maps. The wave of suburban and exurban growth was so massive and so profound, as Tony Hiss observed in *The New Yorker,* that it could be likened to "the work of the great beasts of the last interglacial period, whose browsing destroyed large areas of thick forest."

The first suburban growth wave of the 1950s and 1960s had been accompanied by debilitating white flight and disinvestment, but America's second great suburban migration presented complicated new problems for city residents as development moved ever further away from concentrations of the poor and minorities. Jobs that used to be located downtown were now hours away—via grueling, if not impossible, commutes—from their own inner-city neighborhoods. As the economy boomed in the suburbs and "Help Wanted" signs went up on everything from data processing centers to gas stations, unemployment in the inner city remained stuck in double digits, approaching 40 and 50 percent in some minority communities.

The growth of jobs outside of the city, in places virtually inaccessible by mass transit and where housing was only remotely affordable even for the most well-paid executives, threatened what might be called an "American Apartheid"—a corrosive geographical and social separation of black from white, rich from poor, and opportunity from need. It was a development that demanded public action—concerted regional action from leaders who recognized that such problems transcended every municipal boundary and governmental jurisdiction. Without concerted efforts to repair torn pieces of the metropolitan fabric, the future prospects of every jurisdiction, every neighborhood, and every family across that metropolitan region were in some measure dimmed. Unchecked and ignored, such mindless growth patterns threatened a permanent segregation of America conceivably more intractable and impenetrable than that of South Africa.

## TOWARD NEW URBAN MODELS

Americans have fixated on the ills of their cities for decades, at various times seeking to flee the problems and at other points trying to "solve" them in great bursts of governmental social activism. Yet by the dawn of the 1990s, it was amply clear that national megasolutions were not likely to solve our gnawing neighborhood problems and clearer still that the cut-and-run approach that had been championed by President Reagan would only lead down a long road to national disaster. The federal government was broke. The Department of Housing and Urban Development, created in the 1960s to ride to the rescue of the cities, was paralyzed by internal dissent and paroxysms of corruption, unlikely to get billions of new dollars to provide housing and fix cities. Any kind of national income redistribution scheme to stamp out poverty enjoyed nonexistent prospects in what promised to be years or decades of tight national budgets; nor was there any reason to expect that large social service bureaucracies—whether they were school systems, welfare administering agencies, or housing departments—were at all equipped, on their own, to serve neighborhood and family interests. The evidence, in fact, pointed to the contrary, that megainstitutions more often than not compounded rather than alleviated the problems they were created to address.

In that context, the projects singled out by the Rudy Bruner Award point to vital lessons, potential approaches for the years to come.

**The critical shortcomings of traditional government.** Among these projects there are reminders aplenty of previous government failure, painful illustrations of the shortcomings of the heavy-handed, top-down approach so favored by government at all levels during the 1960s and 1970s. Both Lincoln's Radial Reuse Project and Boston's ambitious Southwest Corridor undertaking, for instance, are literal responses to misdirected public action—in each case abandoned plans to build monstrous roadways that would have torn the very heart from vital urban neighborhoods.

It fell to residents—many of them average working people without any previous involvement in activism or politics—not only to stop the projects but to rescue their communities from the aftermath of the ill-fated government plans. New York City's inspirational TIL housing program stands as a direct rebuke to the inability of the nation's largest city to cope with the country's largest inventory of publicly owned residential property, a response, in effect, to a world-class disaster in a city with world-class housing problems. Portland's critically important 1972 Downtown Plan could only come into being, and flourish, when a very traditionally minded incumbent city planner was eased aside.

We are left with the conclusion that government's inherent conservatism and its frequent alliance with entrenched interest groups represent formidable obstacles. Just as in the successful modern-day corporation, fresh breakthroughs most often have to start with sweeping away a good part of the old—its approaches, coalitions, solutions. Politicians and government officials alike must learn that uncomfortable, sometimes drastic change, a ceding of power to new forces, or at a minimum unprecedented *sharing* of power may well be *essential* if the community is to renew itself.

**The power of decentralization.** In past decades, officials, bureaucrats, and planners were all wed to a mentality of central control. It is a mentality, an approach, that now stands discredited around the world, from corporate boardrooms to the top echelon of governments. Those with their hands on the lever of central authority would have scoffed in the past at the notion that individuals, acting of their own initiative, could produce results in situations that had stymied central government for years. Yet here in the Bruner awards is plain evidence of the fact. In New York City, city-owned housing was and remained a disaster until the city stepped aside and allowed residents to take control of their own lives. No one believes the Boston transportation project could have gone forward without its remarkably decentralized, consultative design. Stowe got its recreational path by "letting go," entrusting the task to one trusted special employee who, in turn, enlisted scores of others. By the same measure, reform can come to a Chicago school system, the Houston police hierarchy, or healthcare systems delivering preventative care through community clinics only if substantial decentralizing, simultaneously *trusting* and *challenging* the constituent parts, becomes a central method of operation. For our society to reach its full potential, to meet its mounting social and physical problems, bureaucrats and planners must step out of the way to allow locally driven solutions to thrive and prosper.

**A new role for government.** Government may not be the sole repository of knowledge and solutions, yet it remains a powerful enabler. As local ecosystems develop to assist communities in finding solutions to housing, economic, recreational, and a host of other problems, the role for government—federal, state, and local—has shifted in critical ways. It is not enough for government simply to "get out of the way." The public sector has a critical role as the pole around which a multitude of interests can rally. Money, of course, is one key. Without a proper level of governmental assistance, few projects can be expected to prosper. Few community efforts—however well-intentioned, even inspired—can be expected to make a dent without the public sector's advice and collaboration on every front, from cash grants to friendly regulation. New York City's TIL program provides a critical illustration of the powerful role of the public sector in providing financing, training, and an overriding framework for community cooperation. The Portland Downtown Plan and Boston's Southwest Corridor testify to the same need—and the greatly increased potential when it is met.

Often the way government helps is by making what could be complex far simpler. Robert Shibley, one of the reviewers and field reporters for the Bruner Award, notes the frequency of "simple organization of complex projects" and uses the Southwest Corridor as an illustration:

> A very simple structure of a task force, assigned by the governor, was established outside the frame of formal power and authority. The task force was then used to influence the various elements and constituencies around the project, face-to-face, in the neighborhoods that had organized to stop the highway. This was done to make a very complex project, the largest capital construction project in the state of Massachusetts, happen. It was a task force of six people. It had one leader, and no formal power or authority other than the governor appointed them to have these conversations. It was a simple organization to run a very complex project. And it worked.
>
> (Robert G. Shibley and Ellen Bruce, eds., *Excellent Architecture: How DO We Know and So What?* Edited transcript of the American Institute of Architects Presentation, May 6, 1989, in St. Louis.)

**The unsung role and power of the invisible bureaucrats.** Without the dedication of behind-the-scenes institutional players and unsung workaday people—the bureaucrats who labor with a project through many, many years and who are often reflexively maligned as faceless governmental apparatchiks—community projects will die on the vine.

In city after city, from Lincoln to New York, progress would never have been possible without the tireless dedication of government officials who excelled, who opened the road to more creative futures, by simply "doing their jobs." Over five years and ten years, sometimes even longer, these are the players who survive the turnover of elected officials, who last through the successions of community leaders who get burned out or who move on to other pursuits. These men and women are not charismatic community activists or powerful politicians. They rarely get public recognition or the public appreciation they deserve. They provide critical institutional stability, however, and they are the glue that holds any successful project together through tough times or sometimes fateful moments.

On occasion, there was the political courage of a public official who helped to make one of these projects possible. One thinks of Massachusetts Governor Francis Sargent, who turned back $650 million in federal highway funds, *hoping* he could get the money back in interstate transfer funds for the Southwest Corridor. In Portland, there was Neil Goldschmidt fighting the bulldozer-happy political establishment in his premayoral days and Governor Tom McCall working assiduously to make Waterfront Park, once the impossible dream, come true.

**The beauty of citizen participation and inclusion.** Citizen participation and inclusion are messy undertakings that often demand infinite patience. Still, without clear and decisive public participation, projects are doomed to failure. Boston's Southwest Corridor would likely have been a design disaster and/or fallen victim to one subsequent budget cutback or another without exhaustive public inclusion, including even late-night sessions to battle out such minute details as the kind of shrubbery to plant along a corridor park in different neighborhoods. Portland's Downtown Plan process practically defined a new, inclusionary mode of bringing citizens "in on the act"—not only creating an enormously important permanent base of citizen understanding and support but transforming the city's mode of decision making in the process. In California's tiny Cabrillo Village, a potentially tragic situation was turned around thanks to the concern and participation of nearly every single resident. The result is a community that was saved and then rebuilt sensitively and sensibly, a model for housing bureaucracies around the nation. The Stowe Recreation Path became reality only through the most painstaking consultation with landowners and local citizens.

There are those who poor-mouth citizen participation, who say it inevitably leads to delays, to stalemates, to wrongheaded compromises. We disagree. There can be negative consequences, but stick with a consultative process long and conscientiously enough and the chances of a positive result are greatly enhanced. When the relevant stakeholders are brought into the action early, and truly heard, and whether the issue is renovating homes or building a park or even getting community agreement for a halfway house, the product is infinitely more likely to be sensitively designed and ultimately successful. Just as vital, consultation is the way to build citizen competence, to make democracy work, to have knowledgeable partners in place when the next major public decision-making process rolls down the pike.

The alternative—stonewalling, secretiveness, attempts to "push one over" on the public—is of course tempting. In isolated cases, such techniques work, but far more often, the result is political embarrassment, delay, higher cost, and, if the project goes forward at all, mediocrity in the ultimate product. This is sure to be increasingly true in the future as the multiple racial and ethnic and income and community groups of America demand a piece of the decision-making pie so often denied them in times past.

**Human empowerment is both a vehicle and a goal.** The ability of people, even the poorest and seemingly most disenfranchised, to seize control, to make a difference, to determine their own lives, and to grab control of their own futures is a critical ingredient of any urban project. Powerlessness leads to frustration which leads to bitterness and antisocial behavior. Empowerment has the opposite and wonderfully positive set of outcomes. New York City's TIL program offers abundant evidence of the blunt power of empowerment of residents, for instance, who were told by their friendly local police to give up, that they would never manage to rid their buildings of the drug dealers who infested every crack and crevice. What the police could not do the residents—energized by the sense of their own potential—managed to accomplish at literal risk to their own life and limb. Welfare mothers—unskilled in the niceties of management theory or bookkeeping—were trained, took over the management of their buildings, and ran them with an efficiency and spirit that paid professionals had never and probably could never hope to have. Many of these same people, having taken control of their own environments, took control of their own lives, confounding the social service bureaucrats who had consigned them and their offspring to lifetimes of dependence on governmental services. They found jobs. They found careers. They realized a potential that the system had refused to acknowledge. In little Cabrillo Village in California, as the residents seized control of a community threatened with oblivion, something curious happened: men who had spent their adult lives working in the backbreaking and often inhumane environment of the fields gained the motivation and the skills to move on to different kinds of work. In a village where high school diplomas were rarities, dozens of teenagers became the first in their families to attend college.

As one of the New York City organizers of the TIL program, who had spent the better part of a decade working with poor New Yorkers to upgrade their living conditions, told us: "People live up to expectations. They're perfect mirrors of the expectations placed on them."

**Individual people with ideas and vision are indispensable—but not always enough.** Often in the 1980s, antigovernment conservatives resorted to the cult of the individual—a community leader (oftentimes a formerly unemployed black woman) who made a project click. In part, it was their way to underscore their arguments about the hopelessness of institutional process. Some of the heroines identified—the likes of Kimi Gray, who organized tenant control of a decrepit public housing project in Washington, D.C., or Bertha Gilkey, who accomplished the same feat in St. Louis—in fact *did* work wonders in returning order, civilization, and a sense of family safety to savaged public housing projects.

In the 1990s and beyond, American society will still need the social pioneers, the stereotype shatterers, but it will also need thousands of ordinary, dedicated men and women, supported and encouraged by government and business and nonprofits alike, to park fresh social initiatives across the continent. The training and creation of successive generations of leaders, people who likely will never garner the publicity of an appearance on "60 Minutes" or be invited to pose beside the president at the White House at the invitation of political image makers, is the explicit goal and lifeblood of such programs as New York City's TIL.

**Design is not the only thing, but it can be everything (or, how for lack of a screw the war was lost).** Sensitivity to design assures that we do not repeat the past, a past in which we built such monstrosities as antihuman housing projects to warehouse people, creating some of the most fearsome social hellholes on the North American continent. Good design, by contrast, shows respect; people accorded respect are far likelier to be contributing, productive citizens. From Boston's Back Bay or Roxbury to rural Stowe, from simple but carefully designed Cabrillo Village to the urban splendor of a redone downtown Portland, sensitive design is paying off.

Good design and a positive *sense of place* go hand in hand. Until America can promise not just social equity but attractive and safe and welcoming places to live for all its citizens, our civilization will be in jeopardy.

For all our nation's faults, these case studies of the Bruner Award, these examples of the *potential* of what our brightest have done and what millions more can do, are a glimpse of a future in which we will all be able to take more pride in being Americans.

CHAPTER 1

# *Home Ownership in New York City's Ravaged Neighborhoods*

A gentle bluff called Sugar Hill rises in northern Manhattan to define the western reaches of Harlem. Approaching the little incline from the south, the wealth and glitter of midtown Manhattan fade slowly, imperceptibly at first, and then faster and faster, much like the fading rays of the sunsets that cast a soft glow on Sugar Hill every night. The towering Empire State and Chrysler buildings become faded afterthoughts. The verdant expanse of Central Park is behind you. The gilded procession of neo-Gothic apartment buildings along Central Park West, with their million-dollar views of the park and the Manhattan skyline, are only vague reference points.

When you are finally upon Sugar Hill, with Harlem baring its battered face and soul to the world, the first thing you notice are the ghosts. Vacant lots are strewn with the sad relics of life. There is a litter of crushed baby carriages, broken bottles, splintered furniture, rusting grocery carts, and burned-out automobiles—even though the landscape is in fact overrun with lush, green weeds that give the place the look of an urban forest. Rows of gutted tenements line the streets. Formerly splendid Tudor and Romanesque buildings are reduced to hulking, haunting presences. Doors are boarded up. Windows are barricaded with bricks and cinder blocks. Graffiti delineate the gang to whom the turf belongs. The occasional curtain fluttering out of otherwise empty windows announces a trace life, a person who has chosen—or been forced—to stick it out. Derelict front porches jog memories of Harlem's Golden Age when these ravaged buildings were home to New York City's black elite—entertainers, professionals, and civil servants.

They all lived on Sugar Hill: on the same streets, in the same scabrous buildings that are now shooting galleries full of junkies and crackhouses erupting in staccato bursts of gunfire with disturbing regularity. This is the same neighborhood where the soothing notes of jazz used to come from old victrolas and the wail of sirens is now as predictable as the rumbling of the subway under the street; where young, violent overlords control entire blocks hawking little vials of crack cocaine to a never-ending procession of people in cars and addicts with vacant eyes; where the lean, angry, modern sounds of rap music punch rhythmic holes into the inner-city air late into the night; where sudden death is only a footnote that does not even merit a mention in the papers; where some grim apartment buildings a stone's throw away mark the expanse of land where a baseball team called the New York Giants once played in a stadium called the Polo Grounds.

These ghosts and spirits inhabit every inch of Sugar Hill, silently tugging at one from every street corner, vacant lot, and front stoop. One asks himself, what went wrong? How could such a thriving neighborhood become a picture postcard for all that has gone wrong in urban America? Then, just as the nightmare of urban rot and abandonment starts overwhelming the senses, little beacons of hope appear and cast some light on the otherwise bleak Harlem landscape.

Hope is very much alive at 676 St. Nicholas Avenue, a building with a shining portico just like the entrances that graced these edifices in the old days. The front of No. 676 has been restored to its former glory. Elderly residents sit in the repainted building lobby keeping interlopers out. The building had gone through five landlords in five years before ending up as city property because of unpaid taxes. The tenants organized, helped put the building back in working order, and finally bought it from New York City. Each tenant paid $250 to buy his or her revised co-op apartment.

The same kind of hope exists just up St. Nicholas Avenue, near the subway stop on the other side of the street. The small apartment building at No. 713 stands out with fresh paint and flowers in the small front yard. All of the ornate trimmings on the building have come alive like old school yearbook photos suddenly brought to life. The basement is littered with construction debris. A tiny laundry room sits with a washer sloshing away in one corner. A few old paintings and some religious icons are scattered about. A little more work, a few more nails, and some Sheetrock™ and the tenants will have a new community room for social activities.

Then there are the human beacons of hope, the people responsible for resurrecting these slices of St. Nicholas Avenue. They are residents who have known Sugar Hill when it swung in its prime

***Hope is very much alive at 676 St. Nicholas Avenue. For the tenants who worked to restore the building, co-ops cost $250.*** *(Photograph courtesy of Hazel Hankin, Brooklyn, New York)*

and when it wallowed at its depths. They are retired black women such as Flora Crane, who moved into 676 St. Nicholas Avenue in 1952 and who remembers the old awning out front and the phone in the lobby to announce visitors. She remembers Sugar Hill when it was a *neighborhood:* a place where people were proud to live, a solid community of working-class people who had never conceived of abandonment or the urban terrorism known as the drug trade. Crane worked for the Federal Reserve Bank of New York for thirty years before retiring. Sitting in the new community room in the basement of her seventy-unit apartment building, she recalls how the drug plague afflicted her neighborhood in the 1970s and how landlords and tenants starting walking away. Sitting there looking elegant, her gray hair neatly coiffed and sporting a dazzling pair of dangling earrings, she remembers the nights when there was no landlord, no heat, no hot water, and little dignity. She describes ceilings that caved in and plumbing that ran like Niagara Falls. She tells of the shattered windows that admitted howling gusts of freezing wind into the building. She describes it so realistically you can feel the cold.

They are women like Katie Fields, who talks about the night a woman froze to death in her building at 713 St. Nicholas Avenue, the rent strike she and other tenants organized in 1973, and their eight-year battle to gain control of their home and their lives. Fields has called Sugar Hill home for forty years. Sitting at the same battered table as her neighbor Flora Crane, she beams as she recounts bringing her building back to life. She and her neighbors have turned their little corner of Harlem around. They have beaten back disintegration, disengagement, and despair. She wants the rest of the world to realize that there is more to Sugar Hill than meets the eye: that there is life—both good and dignified—in her neighborhood. Fields speaks with a restrained force that belies the determination of a person who fights the odds and wins, but her matter-of-fact tone indicates she does not think she has done anything extraordinary. "I get a lot of enjoyment from helping people," she says, smiling. "It makes me feel good to help mankind. I just like to do things. That's what I'm here for."

There are Ozenith Tate, who lives a short distance away at West 143rd Street and Broadway, and Samuel St. George and James Mimms, who live in the same building on East 176th Street in the Bronx. A domestic worker for thirty years, Tate is also at the table in the basement on St. Nicholas Avenue, her gray hair pulled back under her black hat. She is talking about how she spent winter nights with the oven turned up to 350 degrees to warm her apartment after her thirty-one-unit building was abandoned. Most of the residents were old-timers, having lived there for thirty and forty years. Nearly one-third used to be on public assistance. Today, after tenants organized, New York City performed some renovation work, and residents bought their co-op, Tate's building is the pride of her neighborhood. Only one resident is still on public assistance. "It was a matter of pride in owning this piece of property and keeping it clean and planting trees out front," she says. "Those kinds of things lift people's spirits. The tenants really take pride in living there now, and when a conflict arises I invite people into my living room to work things out. I don't mind being available all hours of the day and night."

St. George wears a faded denim jacket. His graying mustache nearly matches the color of the woolen hat he keeps on his head. He and Mimms, who has lived in his Bronx building for forty-one years, have become a kind of Mr. Fix-It duo going from building to building helping residents make repairs. They know they are among the few male leaders in a housing program run largely by women

***Katie Fields, a forty-year resident of Sugar Hill, beams as she recounts bringing her building back to life.*** *(Photograph courtesy of Hazel Hankin, Brooklyn, New York)*

***In this corner of Harlem's Sugar Hill, neighbors have beaten back disintegration and despair with the help of the TIL program.*** *(Photograph courtesy of Hazel Hankin, Brooklyn, New York)*

and they like to joke about it. In 1979, seven of their neighbors in the Bronx banded together and leased their building from New York City. They purchased it in 1982. Mimms remembers the winter nights he spent sleeping in his basement boiler room keeping a balky furnace running so everyone in the building would have heat. One winter St. George took $1,500 from his own savings to buy heating oil for the building. Why do it? Why take on the task of organizing a building with thirty-seven apartments? "We all just wanted some place to live with regular heat and hot water and we decided to stay and fight," Mimms says. "Every time I walk into that front door I feel safe."

Together, St. George and Mimms—both of them schooled in a variety of trades—renovated each apartment in their building. They scraped floors. They put in plumbing and skylights. They painted and plastered. They became so expert in the inner workings of temperamental hundred-year-old apartment buildings that New York City officials started calling on them regularly for assistance. "This is a beautiful experience to me," St. George says. "It gives me great pleasure to call Mister Mimms and say 'Let's go.' We're happy to jump out and help people. I just tell them that once you're settled in you have to go out and do the same thing for other people."

About volunteering all of his time, St. George politely demurs: "I don't care about money," he says. "Money is nothing to me." A former plumber, dishwasher, and then a worker in the garment district for thirty years, St. George underscores the point about money by saying he has all he needs. His savings, to send his son to college, has matured to $26,000. It is all the money he wants.

The odds of fighting for survival in Harlem and the Bronx are tough. Directly behind Flora Crane's haven on St. Nicholas Avenue is a crackhouse where gunfire crackles daily. The abandoned city-owned building sits on Edgecomb Avenue, one of the most notorious drug-dealing corridors in a city full of them. The building is like a running sore, one that the city cannot seem definitively to do anything about. There are so many drug dealers on Edgecomb Avenue that it took three buses to haul off all of the dealers police arrested after one raid. The problems on Edgecome Avenue and elsewhere in the neighborhood remain. Residents angrily charge that some police officers are in cahoots with the drug dealers. They have seen it, they insist. They have seen police officers taking money from the drug dealers rather than arresting them. Flora Crane, Katie Fields, and their friends are indignant about it. The residents of Crane's building hope that the stray bullets that whiz through their windows every now and then do not kill anyone.

Everyone gathered around the table at 676 St. Nicholas Avenue has a story to share about watching the world around them deteriorate and of the remarkable collaboration called the Tenant Interim Leasing (TIL) Program that helped pull their homes back from the brink. Their buildings abandoned by landlords, tenants like Crane and Fields organized their neighbors to run their buildings and ultimately purchased them using TIL, a program that offers training to tenants who want to buy their homes, buildings that have been passed on from speculator to speculator.

These self-effacing heroes offer sharp histories of life and housing in New York City in the post–World War II era that serve as metaphors for all of the daily ills that afflict New Yorkers of average means. They recount the horror of private abandonment, the frustration of public bungling, and the tragedy of life in a city where affordable housing seems only to vanish. They tell inspirational tales of tenant ownership, of human empowerment, and of a program that may be a model for every American city grappling with the problem of affordable housing.

To most Americans, New York City offers a cautionary plot line, one that usually recounts in the impeccable fashion of Murphy's Law what can go wrong, how it happens, and how it is predestined to do so.

However, New York City now has something quite different to offer to the rest of us in the form of the TIL program. It does represent a critical breakthrough in allowing low-income Americans to seize control of their own fate. TIL is compelling. It shows how tenant involvement can be combined with the critical elements of education and training. By letting tenants of abandoned, city-owned buildings buy their homes as co-ops, TIL addresses a set of the most critical problems facing this nation as it enters the twenty-first century: crime, poverty, drug use, social disintegration, and female-headed households. By empowering tenants, TIL offers some guidance not only in rebuilding neighborhoods and homes but in providing a vehicle that allows people to rebuild their own lives. TIL underscores the vital need to keep low-income housing in our cities and of reestablishing a sense of community feeling and sharing.

By the end of 1990, some 356 buildings with 8,500 apartments had been sold to tenants; another 390 buildings with 9,350 apartments were in earlier stages of the process. Only a few buildings have gone back into city ownership since being sold. Tenant associations can take from one to ten years to get through the program; three years is the average. The city intended to renovate and sell 25,000 apartments using TIL during its ten-year housing plan inaugurated in 1986.

One can argue that TIL is one of the few successful *large-scale* attempts, anywhere in the United States, to deal with the seemingly intractable problem of slum housing and the social ills that inexorably accompany it.

## *Decade of Abandonment*

> **One of the few hopes for reversing the disastrous trend toward disrepair and abandonment of sound apartment buildings in this city lies in strong public support of moves by low- and middle-income tenants to assume responsibility for rehabilitating and running the buildings in which they live.**
>
> ***New York Times* Editorial**
> **November 29, 1974**

In the mid-1970s, New York City was staggering back from virtual bankruptcy. Edward Koch was elected mayor in 1977, the same year ABC sportscaster Howard Cosell, calling the play-by-play in the World Series at Yankee Stadium, saw the bonfires of burning buildings in the South Bronx and announced to a worldwide television audience that the Bronx was on fire. Tax money was vanishing. Disinvestment—ranging all the way from the flight of such corporate pillars as Union Carbide and American Airlines to massive housing abandonment by landlords—had gone from a trickle to a steady flow. Much of New York City's affordable housing stock was disappearing, victim to disinvestment, decay, collapse—or all three. What had long been a problem was becoming a full-blown crisis.

Out of such woes came the TIL program. Moratoriums on the construction of new public housing pushed many needy families to the edge of homelessness; they were obliged to move in on top of other families and wait their turn on interminable public housing waiting lists. There were some signs of revival in a number of threatened old working-class neighborhoods, such as Manhattan's Upper West Side and Brooklyn's Park Slope. Redevelopment and the start of "gentrification," however, also removed thousands of apartments from the city's desperately needed supply of low- and moderate-income housing.

At the same time, the wrenching economic changes of the 1970s, brought on by the Arab oil boycott, skyrocketing energy costs, and the restructuring from a manufacturing-based to a service-based economy, were delivering a powerful one-two punch to New York City and its increasingly squeezed middle class.

By the late 1970s, the cost of maintaining and repairing thousands of occupied buildings in the city began to outstrip the income the buildings were capable of producing. Middle-class incomes, however, were nearly stagnant, actually falling in real terms, with inflation in double digits. The "redlining" of entire neighborhoods made it impossible for owners to get insurance or loans for repairs.

Landlords faced a choice: They could operate buildings conventionally, pay bills, and make repairs—but expenses would outstrip the small profit their properties yielded; the cost of providing heat and hot water alone could eat up every penny of rent money and the buildings were no longer viable as long-term investments—or, alternatively, landlords could simply stop making repairs and paying taxes, mortgages, utility, and fuel bills. Sometimes a landlord who still had fire insurance might get "lucky" and have his building consumed by fire.

By letting their property fall to pieces, owners could reap a windfall in the years before New York City foreclosed for nonpayment of taxes. The economics of low-income, inner-city housing were chilling and simple: a few years of neglect and abandonment promised an economic return equal to ten to twenty years of responsible management and investment.

Efforts to force landlords to improve conditions in their buildings and pay their taxes backfired. In 1977, the city seized on what appeared to be a solution. Rather than wait three years to foreclose on properties whose landlords owed money, the city council voted to take ownership after a year. In theory, seizing the buildings earlier in the abandonment process would help turn the tide. Landlords would have a greater incentive to hang on to their buildings if they did not get so far behind on their taxes, and if the city was forced to take ownership, the buildings would not, after a single year of tax delinquency, be nearly as far gone.

The law was well-intentioned but it had a profoundly different effect. Instead of slowing the abandonment syndrome, the city found that it had actually fanned the flames. Thousands of abandoned buildings that were home to tens of thousands of people ended up in city ownership. Speculators sometimes bought and sold buildings in rapid-fire fashion through the "abandonment" process, milking them for fast profits and then returning them to city ownership more deteriorated than before.

Unwittingly, New York City by the late 1970s had become one of the world's largest landlords, owning and managing more than 11,000 buildings—enough property to house the entire population of the city of Hartford. The task of managing this vast portfolio of real estate, spread across all five boroughs, fell to the city's Department of Real Property, an agency experienced primarily in managing commercial real estate.

The South Bronx. Central Harlem. Bedford-Stuyvesant. Washington Heights. The Lower East Side. Wide swaths of New York City were virtually reduced to moonscapes by the cumulative impact of neglect, economics, and bungling. The scope of abandonment in neighborhoods like Harlem, where some 60 percent of the buildings came to be city-owned, was staggering. By 1984, more than 1,500 buildings in the neighborhood with some 22,000 apartments were owned by the city. About two-thirds of them were in central Harlem.

The city's management was haphazard at best, in many cases no better than what the absentee landlords had been doing with the buildings. Some tenants responded to the city's hit-or-miss management of their buildings by taking control themselves. They started collecting rent, making repairs, and forming tenant associations. The tenants did not own the buildings but functioned, for all practical purposes, as if they did.

Andy Reicher, the gregarious, curly-haired executive director of the Urban Homestead Assistance Board (UHAB), a feisty nonprofit set up in 1973 by the Cathedral of St. John the Divine, recalls the

***The scope of abandonment was staggering. In neighborhoods such as Harlem, some 60 percent of the buildings came to be city-owned.*** *(Photograph courtesy of Hazel Hankin, Brooklyn, New York)*

sad comedy of errors that led to the city's housing crisis. UHAB originally provided technical assistance to low-income "homesteaders" to help them rehabilitate and own their homes using a combination of sweat equity, low-interest loans, tax abatements, and cooperative ownership. As the housing crisis mushroomed in the late 1970s, UHAB came to play a central role in designing the TIL program. Reicher put New York City's quandary this way: "The city was the largest slumlord in the world. It had its own management crisis and certainly couldn't manage the buildings. The city needed a way out. People were walking away from buildings on an hourly basis."

A "way out" was what a dedicated group of housing activists devised in 1977 and 1978. After Koch's election in 1977, a number of city council members and housing advocates pushed to establish the Task Force on City-Owned Property. The group included ten community-based organizations plus several council members—all people concerned about the explosion in city-owned housing. The issue: What to do with New York City's residential real estate holdings? Housing advocates saw the moment as a one-time opportunity to develop a program to ensure that these residential buildings would be maintained as affordable housing.

Says Charles S. Laven, who was UHAB's executive director in the 1970s and is now a Columbia University professor:

> We learned that if you can control the definitional language you can control the framework. We defined this as a housing resource, not a problem. In 1978 that was a new way of thinking, but it was quite simple. Who has the most interest in managing this housing stock? The tenants. Can the city manage 10,000 buildings? No. Why not let the tenants do it? Large groups of tenants had already started taking over buildings and were managing in place of a landlord.

Laven drafted the task force's final report, and after much give and take, many of its proposals were accepted by the city's Department of Housing Preservation and Development, which set up a new Division of Alternative Management Programs. The agency's charge was to stabilize and return city-owned buildings to private hands. Up to that point, city-owned buildings were handled in one of two ways: either they were auctioned off, often going to landlords who continued to milk the buildings until the city foreclosed again, or they went into the Central Management Division of the housing department—a status caustically referred to as "purgatory" by tenant advocates.

The report ultimately led to three new housing programs, which were greatly expanded in the mid-1980s as the city crafted an ambitious $5.1 billion, ten-year plan to build 84,000 new units of affordable housing and rehabilitate another 169,000 units:

- **POMP (Private Ownership Management Program).** Under POMP, the city contracts with private real estate management outfits to run, renovate, and buy buildings. The process is quick, requiring only about eighteen months from the start of the POMP contract to the sale of the building to the real estate management firm. As of mid-1990, POMP had sold more than 120 buildings with 4,700 apartments. Another 144 buildings with 4,500 apartments were in the program. The goal under the ten-year plan adopted in 1986 was to renovate more than 31,000 units using POMP.
- **CMP (Community Management Program).** CMP contracts with local nonprofits to prepare, maintain, and manage buildings. The community-based organizations act as intermediaries between contractors and residents. Some community groups have eventually sold their buildings to tenants. CMP is a small-scale undertaking. Under the ten-year housing plan, the city intended to renovate 5,400 apartments using CMP.
- **TIL (Tenant Interim Leasing Program).** Unlike the other two programs, TIL depends entirely on the initiatives and persistence of the residents of a building. *They* must form a tenant association, file a lease with the city, and then show they can manage their building with the rent they collect. If they manage the building successfully for at least two years, the tenant association can buy the building as a low-income co-op. Apartments in the buildings are sold to tenants for $250, a price that was established in the late 1970s. There are resale restrictions to discourage the sale of apartments to more affluent tenants, especially in neighborhoods that experienced gentrification in the 1980s. The co-op owners may, however, keep their apartments if their own incomes increase. While the tenants lease the building, the city government provides specified major repairs and improvements to mitigate emergency conditions.

TIL represents a reversal of the traditional co-op process in which older buildings in newly fashionable neighborhoods are transformed into high-priced apartments, forcing low-income people out.

Details of TIL and the other programs were hammered out in the spring and summer of 1978 and the program started operation later in the year. Laven describes the city as a "recalcitrant partner," particularly when it came to the TIL program, which was slower and messier than some of the other options (the same tension continued into the 1990s as many city officials viewed the faster POMP program as more profitable and more expedient). "On practical grounds they couldn't say no because they didn't know what to do with the buildings if they said no," he says. Listen to Laven's description of the political struggle involved in getting TIL going, however, and the magnitude of the accomplishment begins to set in:

> Opposition at the time came from housing developers as well as bureaucratic centralists and from both the right and left. People on the right argued that the tenants were poor and stupid and couldn't do something complicated like managing a building. They said "Leave it to us." The people on the left argued that housing was a social right appropriately provided by government and that to try and make the poorest people with the least resources provide housing for themselves was, in effect, abusing the poor. The reality was that irrespective of ideology, bureaucratic central control couldn't manage thousands of buildings. . . . So ultimately the ideologues on the right and the left didn't matter. We understood critics on the left and right had good points. When liberals said "You can't leave people without any resources" they were right. And when people on the right said "Running these buildings is a professional job," there was truth in that too. What made the program work was answering both sets of critics.

## *The Beauty of Controlled Chaos*

Look at a map of New York City and TIL buildings show up like clusters of measles outbreaks in Harlem, the South Bronx, Williamsburg, Bedford-Stuyvesant, Clinton, and the Lower East Side. The buildings have temperamental furnaces, octogenarian electrical wiring prone to dangerous short circuits, rotting floors, ancient leaky roofs, and broken windows. Many of them display the accumulated symptoms of a generation of neglect. The smell of urine leaves a foul stench in the halls. Fires have left behind the sickening odor of charred wood. The sour scent of mildew lingers in the air, the cumulative result of water leaks and bad air circulation.

As if the deteriorated physical condition of the apartment buildings did not present enough obstacles, TIL (now New York City's second-largest low-income housing program) also serves people who are poorer and more desperate than the residents of New York City's public housing. When the city looked in the late 1980s, it discovered that more than 60 percent of the households in the buildings it owned were headed by single females; more than half of those families were surviving on incomes below the poverty level and the rest lived in constant danger of joining the official ranks of the poor.

Getting through the TIL program is a long, tough process. Those looking for a neat, pretty program that proceeds according to an established time line need to look elsewhere; there is nothing tidy or ordered about TIL. Each building, set of problems, and group of tenants is different. Most of the time, TIL looks like a bureaucrat's worst nightmare—chaos with only the vaguest outlines of orchestration.

Andy Reicher, the UHAB executive director who studied architecture at the University of California at Berkeley, lives in a TIL co-op. He moved into the twenty-unit tenement on the Lower East Side in 1979 when it was a city-owned building. What he moved into was an apartment that had been inhabited by drug addicts. It was knee-deep in trash. The ceiling had collapsed. There were no windows. Reicher renovated his own apartment. When the TIL program was up and running, the building was the first to sign a lease. TIL, Reicher says, is not for the weak of stomach:

> The essential ingredient of the program is the people. It's hard. There is the conflicting desire of the city to sell and have good record keeping. But the people development process is softer. You *want* people to make mistakes and have the bad experiences during the learning period. It's like learning to ride a bike. The issue isn't whether or not you fall. If a building makes mistakes, say, hires a bad contractor, the question is what do they do about it. If somebody embezzles money, do they deal with it adequately? It's difficult. It's not efficient. It's not neat and clean. This program runs with hundreds of managers and thousands of board members. From the very start you have to let the tenants be in charge. You've got to believe the people in the buildings can do it. It comes across loud and clear if you don't trust them. People live up to expectations. Tenants are the perfect mirrors of the expectations placed on them. People respond to expectations. They're infallible in following them.

Tenant groups with weak leadership or fraught with internal divisions will not survive TIL. The program in fact was deliberately designed to test the mettle of tenant groups by putting some modest obstacles in their way. To get into TIL, buildings have to have at least three apartments and be at least 60 percent occupied. The tenants have to organize at a meeting where they pick officers, from among the residents, to represent the building. At least half the residents have to agree to form the tenant association and to continue paying the current rent or at least $45 per room, whichever is greater. The intent is to have rental income cover the building's operation and maintenance costs. When the tenants sign a lease with the city, they start collecting rent. At a minimum, the building has to be habitable and able to pass a basic safety inspection.

With the tenant association firmly established, the Housing Department's Division of Alternative Management Programs sends in a team of technical staffers to estimate what it will cost to stabilize the condition of the building. The building's officers—who often have no experience in managing an apartment building—must attend classes run by UHAB on such subjects as building and financial management, payroll, and maintenance. Meanwhile, the city conducts an inspection of the building, trying to identify along with the tenant association exactly what repairs are needed to hold the building together for ten to fifteen years. The tenants create the repair plan, set priorities, put together a budget, and identify the repairs they can do themselves.

The city-financed rehab work focuses on major "system" repairs—fixing and replacing boilers, roofs, and electrical systems. In the early 1980s, the city budgeted an average of $2,000 to $5,000 per unit to do the renovation work; by the early 1990s, it was spending up to $15,000 per apartment to rehab buildings. (The increased costs were partly the result of more thorough repair plans and partly because buildings coming into the program in the late 1980s and early 1990s were in far worse condition and in need of more repairs than earlier buildings.)

As TIL's political star rose, so did its budget. In the mid-1980s, the city spent an average of $11 million a year on the program. In 1989, the budget was increased to $21 million; by 1990, the city was spending $28 million on TIL. New York City was increasing its overall commitment to affordable housing in the wake of a decade that had brought increased economic polarization to the city and a virtual federal abrogation of a role in social programs.

Reagan-era budgets had brought extraordinarily deep cuts in federal low-income housing money—roughly 60 percent overall. As the George H. Bush administration assumed office and Jack F. Kemp took over as secretary of the U.S. Department of Housing and Urban Development, the agency got bogged down in a major corruption scandal that slowed attempts to reorient federal spending. Federal money had provided nearly three-fourths of the money to run TIL in the late 1970s; by the early 1990s, Uncle Sam's share was 25 percent and shrinking. Even so, TIL had turned into a good deal for New York City, becoming the least subsidized of all its housing programs. Every apartment that the city still managed directly cost at least $2,000 per year. The comparable average subsidy in the TIL program, by contrast, was only $500.

It took the city about six months to arrange the transfer of buildings to tenant control, including formulating the repair plan, and another eighteen months or so to perform repairs. One persistent problem with TIL that often comes back to haunt tenant groups after they have purchased their buildings is shoddy repair work done by loosely supervised city contractors who must be hired on the basis of lowest-bid contracts. Tenants often give up on the city and do as much of the repair work as they can afford to do themselves. "We fixed up our building and did it with our own money," says Katie Fields of St. Nicholas Avenue. "We try to deal with good, reliable contractors. The city contractors are the worst in the world."

Once a tenant association has proved its competence and shown that it can collect at least 85 percent of the rent, a building can go into the "sales pipeline." Many buildings never make it as far as the sales process, according to Joan Wallstein, the assistant commissioner of the housing department and the city official who oversees the TIL program. Selling is another long, cumbersome procedure that can range from six months to a year. The sale has to be certified by various city agencies. The agreement to purchase has to be signed by at least 60 percent of the building's tenants. About ten or twenty sales are completed every year.

To discourage resale of low-income co-op units, the city limits profits tenants may realize. For the first ten years, any profit has to be divided between the seller and the co-op. In 1982, after a long political fight, the city decided that it would get 40 percent of all profits from any resale of a co-op. The seller and the co-op would divide the remaining profits. So far, there have not been a lot of resales—if for no other reason because there are precious few housing alternatives for low-income New Yorkers. Even if someone qualifies for public housing, there is a waiting list of 175,000 people for 170,000 occupied apartments.

Tenant initiative, according to all parties to TIL, has been one of the keys to its success and a critical reason tenants have been required to do the legwork to organize themselves and inquire about the program. Tenant initiative is a very important part of the program because it is not easy to manage a multiple-dwelling building or even to live in a co-op without a lot of resources, says Wallstein:

> These aren't people with resources or background in management. There has to be a whole lot of will to make it work. It's miraculous that you find that will and the will to work together on the tough problems of managing the buildings.

Wallstein has been an assistant housing commissioner since 1981. Her bright office in lower Manhattan has a picturesque view of the Brooklyn Bridge and the South Street Seaport. The calm of her office and her own reserve contrast sharply with her description of the chaotic nature of TIL. According to Wallstein:

***Unlike other city programs that have addressed Harlem's housing crisis, TIL succeeded by depending on the initiative and persistence of the residents.*** *(Photograph courtesy of Hazel Hankin, Brooklyn, New York)*

TIL started with inadequate staff. The first group of buildings were the ones out there chomping at the bit to get a chance to manage themselves. We were taking in as many buildings as we could. Went from zero to three hundred buildings very quickly. The feeling was that the tenants were coming to us and that the first hurdle they had to get past was to come to us and say they wanted to take part.

For a long time there wasn't enough money to do enough physically for the buildings. We didn't have the money to carry out a repair plan from beginning to end. It wasn't until 1988 [ten years after TIL started] that we started to have the resources we needed. In the beginning it was all federal money. As time went on and that dried up, the city started trying to fill the gap. There probably still isn't as much money for training as there ought to be, but it's a question of resources.

It's really incredible that the people in these buildings are doing as good a job managing the buildings as they are. These are people with no background in management who've learned by trial and error how to do it. Many of them are quite expert at it.

## *The Nuts and Bolts of Life*

> **We are trainers. We teach the how-tos of building management—from bookkeeping to decision making. But the tenants are the doers. They are the ones who . . . build upon the dedication and vision they already have and then upgrade *their* buildings, *their* communities, and *their* lives. The result: strengthened communities through co-operative ownership and involvement by residents.**
>
> ***Self-Help in Our Own Words:***
> ***UHAB, Our First 15 Years***
> **(New York: Urban Homestead Assistance Board, 1989)**

On a rainy Manhattan evening, there is a lot of activity in the modest, messy web of UHAB offices on Prince Street on the northern fringes of Little Italy. Outside, the steady downpour is keeping the streets quiet. Inside, sitting at college-style desk chairs around a white-walled meeting room, about two dozen people—black, white, and Hispanic—are taking part in a classroom seminar on the nitty-gritty of running co-op apartments.

The "students" are a mixed lot. Most of them are women. Tenants, tenant leaders, and UHAB staffers alike are taking part in the exercise, clinically known as the Small Group Activity Method. The procedure is instructive in getting at what makes TIL tick. The students break into groups of three and four and start talking about theoretical problems in their buildings. As the discussion progresses, it becomes painfully obvious that the "theoretical" problems trainers are posing to the class are real dilemmas. The first task the trainees are assigned is to suggest how they would cope with tenants who pay rent but otherwise do not become involved in building activities.

All of the participants in one group agree that getting more tenants involved in their buildings is a problem. They sit casually chatting and joking. Alverine Roberts of the 724 East 216th Street Tenants Association complains that getting people to participate is a tough job. "No matter how much you talk and talk to people, it goes in one ear and out the other," she says.

"Damn right," another young woman in the group chimes in.

The tenants and trainers run through an entire list of obstacles: the work schedules of tenants, the need for child care, basic lack of interest on the part of some, tenants who feel alienated or left out from the group. "People feel they have their own problems," Roberts says. "Why should they deal with these other problems?"

It is only a warm-up exercise. UHAB trainers follow up by handing out a sheet describing the problem of subletting apartments in TIL co-ops. As the apartments become more and more valuable on the open market, tenants start coming up with dozens of ways to circumvent requirements designed to preserve them for low- and moderate-income tenants. Everyone around the room silently studies the sheet. A sample problem: One building has a tenant who owes $5,000 in back rent. The apartment is occupied by a nephew who is subletting the unit from his uncle for $400 a month. The uncle is actually supposed to be paying $100 a month in rent but he pockets the $400 a month and does not even fork over the official rent. After much discussion around the room, the students come up with some approaches to stop the subleasing problem. Their answers center on monitoring who is moving in and out of the building plus setting up a formal subletting procedure.

The session continues for three hours into the evening. The subleasing discussion is followed by sessions on how to deal with tenant anger, the problem of nasty residents, and procedures that are necessary to keep communications open in a building.

Such training sessions, which are both the key to and genius of the TIL program, are run by UHAB using funds the city has provided to offer management training and technical assistance. UHAB runs the training seminars and also has produced an entire curriculum of printed material in both English and Spanish on subjects ranging from building management skills and rent collection to financial management and self-governance. (The materials contain clever cartoon-style illustrations and are a model of how to communicate complex material to people not frequently confronted with such information.)

Tenants are even taught how to get through New York City's byzantine housing court system. UHAB field workers make regular visits to buildings in the program. Staff members are, in fact, encouraged to live in TIL buildings themselves as long as they meet the income requirements. "We live this stuff every day," says Ann Henderson, a UHAB administrator who lives in a homesteading building in East Harlem. "We all know what it's like to live with your neighbors as cooperative members."

The first TIL building was sold to tenants in 1980. In 1981, the city, UHAB, and the New York Community Trust set up the Cooperative Support Program to provide aid to new co-op owners. The program helps co-ops monitor their progress and aids their boards in locating government and private initiatives that could help low-income co-ops. It has a standing "Emergency Loan Program" under which co-ops that cannot qualify for bank loans can borrow money for up to twenty years at a 3 percent interest rate. The program also helps the co-ops remove building code violations, which can cost up to $100 in fines per violation per day. It assists them in obtaining city tax abatements, which allow them to make capital improvements with no tax assessment increase for twenty years. The program also offers a prepaid legal assistance program and fire and liability insurance.

Tenants and administrators alike say the training and follow-up are critical since few of the tenants joining the program have the necessary managerial, accounting, engineering, and political skills to run apartment buildings. Ozenith Tate, who was an early entrant into the TIL program in the late 1970s, remembers the challenges posed at first by a program that did not offer complete training:

> It was like putting the cart before the horse. There wasn't a great big training program. I don't know anything about managing a building. There was no school you could go to to learn. The city was telling us we're going to own and run a building. A third of the people are on public assistance. It's an 80-year-old building. Most of the tenants are women and women are running the building. There was a lot of paperwork that most of us didn't understand. You have to be an engineer, a lawyer, and an accountant.

Tate and her neighbors found the training made available immensely valuable in running their building, with its need for massive repairs and a relatively tiny pool of money. "You don't have to be a college graduate to participate," she says. "You just have to be willing to learn and work at it and there's all kinds of assistance for you."

Andy Reicher notes on the same front:

> Training and ongoing assistance are the essential ingredients. You can't just do the rehab work, throw a party and say "Here, it's your home now." That doesn't work. You need to do the rehab work but the physical environment really has little to do with ultimately succeeding. Developing co-ops and viable long-term housing alternatives that enable and empower residents and that are resilient in the long run is a people-building process, not a brick and mortar program.

Listening to Reicher describe the guts of the TIL program, one gets a clear sense that New York City has something quite valuable to teach the rest of the nation and the federal government as it casts about for new approaches to housing policy:

> A lot of the learning we've gone through isn't widely understood. Many of the models for tenant management—in Washington, D.C., in St. Louis—are really built on charismatic leadership. That is great for getting things started, but it's disastrous in the long run. We're looking for sustainable, long-term leadership. The leadership should be anonymous and change every few years. The federal government is guilty of committing the cult of the individual. It increases the potential problems and has noth-

ing to do with the adequacy of management, dispersion of skills, or competence. The long-term viability is in management systems, ongoing support, retraining, and education. It's not flashy rehabs. [HUD Secretary] Jack Kemp should be running around teaching bookkeeping.

## *Miracles on Rivington Street*

Approaching Rivington Street from the west, you traverse the entire spectrum that is New York City's Lower East Side. You skirt the northern edges of SoHo and its procession of gentrified affluence—boutiques, art galleries, bars, performance spaces, and lofts. You walk through the remnants of the old European mélange that was the Lower East Side, passing the occasional Polish or Ukrainian shop or restaurant, the old sign in Yiddish that hangs in the window like a billboard from another planet, and then those immigrants' latter-day successors in the neighborhood—Salvadorans, Puerto Ricans, Dominicans, and Jamaicans.

Treading your way through the human wreckage lining the Bowery, you jog across a little park that is sometimes filled with the sounds of children playing and at other times bursts with the street language of drug dealers. Suddenly you are upon Rivington Street, predominantly Hispanic and alive with the sounds of Latino music and the smells of Central American cooking. Healthy commerce presses hard against burned out and abandoned buildings, forming a little checkerboard pattern of life and deterioration all sharing the same space on the same street.

The twenty-four-unit apartment building at 46 Rivington Street does not have a doorman, awning, or fancy vestibule. The number "46" is scrawled on the front door in thick black Magic Marker. Inside, the building has a utilitarian look. The cinder-block walls are painted white and the new lighting casts enough light on the halls to reveal plasterwork and a paint job that would not pass muster uptown.

Jim Pender, the middle-aged, bearded treasurer of the co-op at 46 Rivington, is sitting in his modest apartment wearing a worn tan jacket. He keeps a pencil tucked behind one ear and is fidgeting with a rubber band wrapped around his wrist. The apartment is not messy, just cluttered. It has a bunk bed for Pender's two children, and toys are scattered around.

Since the late 1970s, he and his neighbors have cleaned their building, evicted a small army of drug dealers, and made their building habitable again. Pender, who has a slight build, was beaten up for his trouble. He was threatened. Some of his neighbors were also threatened. Leaning back on a rickety chair, he is nonchalant about the experience.

When Pender moved into the building in the early 1980s, his wife was pregnant. "This was the only place we found with walls, a ceiling, and windows," he says of his move to New York City from Baltimore. "We were new to the city, and I guess we were a little bit naive." Pender's welcome wagon came within ten minutes when he realized that a small drug supermarket was operating across the hall. A procession of people came and went from the apartment door, knocking, passing money through a peephole, and taking small packets with drugs away. He discovered that sixteen of the twenty-four apartments in the building were involved in drug trafficking. The police pointed out to him that he was living in one of the most drug-infested buildings in the neighborhood. They asked him why he was living there.

Pender was not living on Rivington Street for long before the city took control of the building because the landlord was behind on paying taxes. Everything in the building was breaking down. There was a period of time when the residents did not even know the city was running the building. After finding out about the new management, some of the tenants tried to get the city to make repairs. The housing bureaucracy declined. "The city people were afraid of what they saw," Pender recalls with a thin smile. "They refused to make any repairs."

And so, some tenants of 46 Rivington started collecting the rent themselves while trying to hold the building together. About half of the residents cooperated. Pender recalls:

> There were still people left here who wanted to make their lives better and the building safer and cleaner. The guy who started it was a Dominican and most of the residents were Dominican. He used his suasion to convince everyone that we could do it. . . . We recognized that we had to collect as much as we could to make repairs and we started to use legal means to make people pay.

At the same time, the tenant activists in the building started trying to evict drug dealers who were using their apartment as shooting galleries. As Pender describes it:

> There were no niceties like a formal tenant selection process. The idea was to get the bad guys out and the good guys in as fast as we could.

A number of dealers were thrown out by New York City's housing court because they did not pay rent, and in 1984, 46 Rivington entered the TIL program.

Slowly but surely, some desperately needed, massive repairs were made. The boiler was replaced. New bathrooms were installed. Plumbing that sent leaks cascading through the building was repaired. The tenants started replacing refrigerators, stoves, and shelving in the apartments. The junkies and drug dealers left or were kicked out, one by one. The building stabilized and the tenants bought it in 1988. As the realization dawned on residents that they had the chance to own their own homes, they began taking more care of the building and their own apartments. After the sale was completed, individual co-op owners started making expensive repairs to their own units. "People now go out of their way to do little things and watch out for the building," Pender says. "Now most everyone keeps their apartment doors open. It's like an extended family." The majority of the tenants in the building are Dominican. English is spoken in only four apartments, counting Pender's.

The story Pender tells is uplifting—it is not hard to sense the energy that he and his neighbors brought to turning their building around. The results are excellent, but the question remains: Why literally risk life and limb to stay in a building that was falling apart? Why not move?

"You start to think of it as your home," Pender answers firmly. For the first time, his cynical humor lifts and he displays a genuine trace of anger, a twitch of the brow that belies deeper feelings:

> You're here with your family. It belongs to you as much as it does to anyone else. You get morally indignant. There were lots of people who deserved a good chance and a few people that were keeping the rest of us from having that chance. Without TIL the building would have burned down. All the other buildings on the block around here were torched.

There is a knock at the door. A tenant walks into Pender's apartment, rent check in hand. The sounds of children playing in the hall filter inside the apartment. Pender had been working for eight years as a full-time cook at a nearby restaurant, in addition to putting in about thirty hours a week helping to run his building. He is unemployed for now and says that he has been enjoying the chance to take classes "and be a house husband" while his wife works. "My job is to keep up with the different bureaucratic things you need to follow with the city and all of the repair people that come and go," he says. "I've been involved in the building longer than anyone else now."

The changes on Rivington Street in the last decade have been dramatic. On a pleasant day in 1990, the drug trafficking that once plagued the entire street is nowhere in evidence. The building at No. 46, once a lonely outpost of civility, is no longer alone. Even the hulking ruin directly across the street, a building that was abandoned and wrecked in the early 1980s, is poised to come back to life. In some neighborhoods, the residents would be putting up a stink. The building would be turned into a hospice for patients dying from AIDS. On the western end of Rivington Street, the coming of the hospice is yet another sign of progress.

Just a short walk from Pender's building is 175 Rivington. Jose Augusto, jolly and barrel-chested, is the superintendent of the building. He shares with Pender the distinction of being a middle-aged man in a program dominated by older women. Augusto grew up in this neighborhood before moving to Puerto Rico with his family when he was fifteen years old. When he came back to New York City, he went back to the old neighborhood, to a building that he knew was seriously deteriorated and faced severe troubles. "We were looking for an apartment," he says. "We knew we were moving into a building with problems, but we knew we just had to get the problems out and get the building up and going."

As Augusto described the trials and tribulations of the place he calls home, a gut rehabilitation was well under way at the twenty-six-unit apartment building housing a small bodega (Hispanic grocery store) on the ground floor. Half of the apartments had been finished, and the building buzzed with construction activity. Construction trash lined some hallways. Some walls were stripped down to wooden studs. Sawdust and a thin coating of plaster dust coated most exposed surfaces. The smell of fresh paint was everywhere in the darkened halls where lighting fixtures were being torn out and replaced. In one apartment, workers were starting work on a new drop ceiling. Another apartment on the top floor looked like a hand grenade had been set off inside, par for the course in serious renovation work. Plumbing fixtures were laying at odd angles on the floors. An entire wall was missing, replaced temporarily by a big sheet of plastic.

A work in progress, 175 Rivington was a project highlighting some of the trials and tribulations that participants in TIL face as they try to get their buildings in shape to buy them. The difference between the renovated and old apartments is staggering. In the unrenovated apartments, dirty floors clash with peeling paint and antiquated bathroom fixtures compete with ancient kitchen appliances for the title of being the most outmoded. In the fixed-up units, floors shine, walls sport bright coats of paint, and the appliances looked as though they had been plucked right off a showroom floor.

Augusto conducts the tour of 175 Rivington like a maestro proud to show off his accomplishments. There is a twinkle in his eyes as he opens the door to reveal a newly finished apartment, and there is always a hearty laugh when he describes a little victory the tenants won in their fight to reclaim their building.

Listening to Augusto tell the story of his building, when he is back at his desk in the building manager's office, is a little like taking a Jeep ride down a bumpy highway. A Hispanic community group had been running the building in the early 1980s. "The tenants were fighting all the time," he says. The community group "wasn't doing nothing," he says, except presiding over further deterioration in the building. In 1983, a group of tenants decided they were going to run the place themselves.

"We decided we were going to live like human beings," Augusto says. "To do that, we knew we were going to have to fight." It was just the start of the struggle at 175 Rivington. First came the people problems in the buildings—not just the drug dealers but apathy on the part of tenants as well. "All of us were in it together," Augusto says with a wide, sweeping motion of his hands, "but the people in the building would say that they paid their rent and that's where their responsibility stopped. Some people in the building were interested in moving ahead. Without everybody involved, you can work for years and it's tough."

The biggest step was ridding the building of drug dealing. Augusto reaches into his desk drawer and pulls out a special security key for the front door. He explains:

> When we had regular keys people made copies, and the drug problem was bad. We had a lot of confrontations. One dealer we confronted in the hallway laughed at us and told us we'd never have a chance. But we got the building clean. Yeah, people got mad. They start threatening you. I got threatened. But we threatened the dealer back. We took them to court. We brought in the cops. We gave a key to a cop who'd come around. The trouble is the police start something and don't continue. So we knew we were on our own. Thank God we don't have the problem anymore. If you let the problem go it's like a cancer. If you don't take care of it, it will kill you.

There was the tenant association treasurer who fouled up the books so badly that bills were not paid and it was impossible to keep track of finances; not to mention the tenant association vice president who sold marijuana professionally before he was hounded into leaving. By 1990, however, most of the "problem" tenants had been routed—except one, and residents were hard at work on that one, too. Augusto plunks a file full of reports on his desk about the tenant, a formerly homeless woman placed in the building by the city. He and the other residents say she is an alcoholic. In January, she set her apartment on fire. Augusto holds up a photo of a charred bed and tosses it back down. She broke a $300 window because she had lost the door key. He reaches for a petition and counts out the twenty-two signatures—one by one—asking the city to remove her from the building. "She's the only problem we have now," he says.

Then there was the city of New York and the TIL program, which provided the money and contractors to replace the boiler, rewire the building, and fix the outside of the building. Augusto has words of praise for the program itself but pans the city's performance. Residents "had to fight" the city to start making repairs in the building, he says, and "all the city wanted to do was to sell the building fast. They were paying contractors a lot of money to do a bad job." The tenants are now using the $8,000 a month they collect in rental income to do the renovations in the apartments themselves. "The city is fixing apartments for $18,000 and we're doing it for $10,000," he boasts, jutting out his chest. He laughs to make the point. "The apartments look like Fifth Avenue. That's what we want."

Augusto is so proud of his building he insists on showing off the roof. On a crystal-clear day with a fresh breeze blowing up from New York Harbor, the view is spectacular. The twin towers of the World Trade Center loom to the south, the Empire State Building to the north. To the east is a spaghetti tangle of bridge approaches and the Williamsburg Bridge. Augusto motions toward the rotting building next door. There are gaping holes in the charred roof that let you see clear through several floors. He laughs again. "We want to get that building," he says. "We want to run it. When you get out of this program you can run five buildings. We can get good people into this neighborhood who want to work to improve it."

There is ample evidence in New York City that TIL has improved individual lives, buildings, and communities. Buildings have been cleared of the plague of drug dealers. Individual residents have picked up skills, such as finance and property management. Stories abound of residents who were on public assistance and found jobs after their buildings went through TIL. Says Lee Farrow, UHAB's director of the Cooperative Support program:

> When you start to open new horizons, when people begin to realize that they can actually do things, it doesn't just stop. They venture into other areas. They go on to other buildings, to community groups. They go into the political world and become more politically motivated and aware, and that exceeds what we're doing, in a sense, because it gives people who were never politically aware a chance to stop and say, "I have a decision in this world. I can make a decision, and I'm going to profit from it."

Independent experts who have looked at the program have come to similarly striking conclusions. Jacqueline Leavitt and Susan Saegert, two sociologists who interviewed more than one hundred residents of TIL buildings, concluded that many of the co-ops had developed "community households" to share the econonmic and managerial burdens.

In *From Abandonment to Hope: Community-Households in Harlem* (Columbia University Press, 1990), they wrote:

> Tenants in . . . co-ops exhibited a sense of empowerment that contrasted strongly with the psychological sense of abandonment conveyed by many, especially of the elderly tenants, in buildings brought back from abandonment by community or private landlords. . . . Tenants in co-ops rated their housing as physically better, better managed, and more satisfactory. They reported more attachment to their homes and more cooperative relationships with other tenants. They participated more in the upkeep of the buildings.

Leavitt and Saegert also found that the TIL program had a profound effect on elderly and female tenants who, more often than not, functioned in leadership roles in their buildings. The residents, they concluded, "had taken control of their lives and their buildings in a situation that still befuddles even the most intelligent urban scholars and policymakers."

Although they live at opposite ends of Manhattan, in different worlds, and come from different generations, Ozenith Tate of Harlem and Jose Augusto of the Lower East Side come to similar conclusions about a program that has much to teach policymakers around the nation.

"Everybody is looking for ways to house poor people," Tate said in the Harlem basement on St. Nicholas Avenue. "This program will work if you can inspire enough people. I really have a good feeling about it. We're proud of what we've done."

Back up on his roof, Augusto looks at some of the other buildings in his neighborhood and shakes his head. "I don't know how people used to live here," he says. For one of the first times, the ever-present smile leaves his face. "I just don't know how people lived here. We'll never let it slide back."

If it can happen in the multiheaded bureaucratic, cultural, and economic hydra called New York City, one has to believe it can happen anywhere in the United States.

## *Commentary: New York City*

POLLY WELCH: Government tends to look at shelter as programmatically separate from social services, but they are inextricably connected. Progress in one, as in the TIL program, may offset costs in another. I am curious as to whether the TIL residents have reduced their dependence on welfare. TIL may have outcomes on other government programs, such as reducing costs, that aren't being quantified. People are using their new skills to find a job or to help others in the community, which can't help but reduce their dependence on other programs.

**ROBERT SHIBLEY:** There's an odd bottom line in that question of whether TIL tenants have reduced their dependency on welfare. There are lots of structural reasons that people are either unemployed or underemployed and therefore dependent on social services. To make a program of self-help housing responsible for getting people off welfare in the face of the structural conditions that put them there in the first place is asking too much.

**DAVID LAWRENCE:** Still, I bet the positive results are there. TIL is the story of individuals seizing an opportunity to control their housing and receiving satisfaction from that responsibility. The broader effects are intangible until they are quantified. It makes me wonder what the future impact is. This chapter gives the micro picture but we also need more of the macro picture. The full potential of a program like TIL is staggering.

**SHIBLEY:** A theme that is resonant here is the marriage between an explicit and concrete recognition of the importance of training and the method of training. This is not the training model of "sit down, shut up, and take notes." TIL builds on the assumption of competence and good will on the part of the people involved.

That fundamental assumption didn't exist in any of the other housing models available to New York City when they started these conversions. It's not part of the standard framework. The old assumption was that you had to buy competence. The old message to potential tenants was: "We expect you to be incurably incompetent in the skills necessary to manage this housing. All we can do is try to staff this place with slightly higher class personnel who, because we've employed them, can afford to pay for it." As opposed to this old assumption, TIL engages those underemployed and unemployed people and gets them to do it for themselves, and "doing it" ranges from managing buildings to knowing how to fill in a check to pay a bill on a regular basis.

**WELCH:** I am skeptical about motivations here. If developers feel that TIL takes away prime property in a hot real estate market they may pressure city government as owner to let a building's vacancy rate fall below 50 percent and sell it off as vacant property, thus avoiding the TIL program. If a building is less than 50 percent occupied, its residents can't join the program.

LAWRENCE: I don't think it works that way in practice. The New York City government may not realize it, but one of the things it's best at is following the path of least resistance. The issue becomes: Is the path of least resistance to simply allow occupancy to fall or is it to find ways for the city to rid itself of burdensome properties that it can't adequately manage? I think it's the latter. There is so much property!

WELCH: One of my concerns about the federal government's interest in expanding self-help co-op programs is that it tends to see them as one-shot deals. These programs require a sustained advocacy, as this chapter illustrates. There are always new problems—a change in the insurance law or banking regulations or leadership—that may require expertise or resources that the residents don't have. Washington doesn't recognize this when HUD [Department of Housing and Urban Development] speaks of selling low-income housing to residents.

LAWRENCE: What we've learned about leadership is important here. There are not enough charismatic leaders to deal with all the buildings in the TIL program, and the difficulties and duration of the TIL process are such that no leader could survive the natural diminishing of charisma that occurs over time. You need a grassroots effort where three or four or more people look at each other and say: "I guess it's up to us to do it. We'll each take a piece of it and get it done."

WELCH: This chapter describes alternatives to the myth of the charismatic leader. TIL has created communities of people who act together by consensus for the collective good. HUD Secretary Jack Kemp has missed this key component of self-help housing by celebrating the individual behind some of these projects. That's very misleading. The strength of the Rudy Bruner Award is that it considers a project's ability to sustain itself. Most of the finalists have achieved success by the collective and cooperative action of many people.

SHIBLEY: There are so many people in need that, if they were supported properly, TIL could provide a very viable alternative to the private ownership model—with much longer term benefits and with much greater results in producing affordable housing, but you've got to create a support network for those folks. UHAB in contract to the city has been that support system. The training loop is built into the contract. It's also important that UHAB draws its staff from TIL building tenants. They've been through the cycle and have seen it work.

The TIL program makes historical adversaries into collaborative advocates. It takes the stereotype of the city as the bad guy and the housing advocate as the good guy (or the other way around depending on your politics) and puts them together in the same project, producing successful results. It doesn't always have to be a fight with city hall, it can be a dance. It's not an easy dance—there are bruised toes—but a dance nonetheless.

CHAPTER **2**

# *Portland's 1972 Downtown Plan: Rebirth of the Public City*

There is a rare magnificence to Portland's setting in the Northwest rain forest of America. Sited at the head of the lush green valley of the Willamette River, just before it reaches its confluence with the mighty Columbia, the Oregon city is all but surrounded by mountains. To the west rises the Coastal range and to the east the Cascades. On a clear day, Portlanders have a stunning view of Mount Hood, rising serene into the heavens. Oftentimes mist settles in a band below Hood's summit, leaving the mountain's great white peak floating, as it were, on the horizon.

Traditionally, Portland was viewed as a prim, proper city, true to the New England roots of its first settlers. It was from its early years a town of independent farmers, loggers, and seamen, along with captains of business and industry, but Portland never took on the character of a San Francisco with its Gold Rush or a Seattle with its Klondike adventurers and bitter labor wars. Asians and blacks joined Portland's New Englanders, but contentious ethnic politics never took root here. Oregon became a kind of pilot station for early-twentieth-century Progressive-era governmental reform, and as environmentalism became a recognized national value, Portland was ready to embrace and even embody it.

There are, in fact, few cities so at home with their natural world. Trees grace almost every Portland street; greenery adorns most buildings. There are ten parks in downtown Portland alone. The city has some 7,000 square miles of parkland, including wilderness areas and wildlife sanctuaries and the trails of a forty-mile loop that was proposed back in 1903 by the famed park planner brothers, John Charles and Frederick Law Olmsted, Jr.

Along the loop, all within the city's borders, one can find nature refuges teeming with more than 140 species of birds, from belted kingfishers to song sparrows to red-shouldered hawks to black-billed magpies. Portland's official bird is the great blue heron. Two heron rookeries are within the city. With their long plumes and blue-gray plumage, the adult herons add special excitement as they soar over the Willamette and past downtown skyscrapers.

Vegetation flourishes in the moist coastal climate zone, and Portland, for each June since 1909, has celebrated its now famous Rose Festival. The city's taste for naturalness extends to its public places: consider "Ira's Fountain" (after civic leader Ira C. Keller), a place that a wandering *New Yorker* correspondent chose to call "neither entirely a park, nor merely a fountain." It consists of a series of man-made "waterfalls" in which 13,000 gallons a minute cascade over rocklike cliffs into a sunken pool. There are terraced steps and platforms to draw the pedestrian even behind the falls. Great trees overlook the scene. This park, one of two San Francisco architect Lawrence Halprin executed in downtown Portland, was described by the *New York Times'* Ada Louise Huxtable as "one of the most important urban spaces since the Renaissance." Whatever its national accolades, it is most surely one other thing: a shared delight of Portlanders of all ages and backgrounds.

Neither "Ira's Fountain" nor the Rose Festival nor the forty-mile loop nor Portland's hospitality to blue herons has any official link to Portland's receipt of the Rudy Bruner Award for Urban Excellence. The award went officially for the city's 1972 Downtown Plan, the process by which Portland gathered broad community consensus and set its vision for two decades of remarkable inner-city planning and progress. Portland's civic culture, with its traditions of quiet respect between players on the urban scene, of openness to experimentation and planning, of outdoor naturalness, and a sense of conserving the best of physical and social environments alike, would prove to be fertile soil in which the Downtown Plan could grow and succeed.

The 1972 Downtown Plan had its roots in crisis: deep concern that Portland was losing its traditional commercial and residential markets to fast-growing suburbs and that it might cease to be the economic, cultural, and social center of its region. In the words of Gregory Baldwin, an urban planner/designer and major player in Portland developments of the past two decades:

> The specific object was to create an urban community sufficiently attractive as a place to encourage citizens and activities in the immediate region to concentrate their energies and resources in the downtown. [The goal] was simply to make downtown Portland the best place to be.

Numerous achievements are claimed for the plan, and they are hard to dismiss:

- The $500 million of public investment made between 1972 and 1986 leveraged $1.7 billion of private investment in downtown Portland.
- Downtown employment grew by 30,000 and total assessed property value increased 382 percent.
- The downtown retail district increased its penetration of the regional retail market from 7 percent to more than 30 percent of dollar volume sales—the diametric opposite of the trends almost everywhere else in America.
- A handsome expanse of green waterfront park, running from the edge of downtown buildings to the shores of the Willamette, replaced an ugly riverside expressway that had isolated the river from the city.
- To meet the plan goals of increased public access to downtown, historic transit advances were made. A bus transit mall, completed in 1978, opened along Fifth and Sixth avenues, serving the city's high-density spine. Then, in September 1986, came the first line in a regional light rail system, passing through downtown and extending to Gresham, fifteen miles to the east. Cumulative results: transit trips into downtown increased from 79,000 daily in 1975 to 128,000 daily in 1985. Transit's share of commuter trips into downtown went up from 28 percent to 52 percent.
- Radically revised planning guidelines required a "terracing" of building heights from the center of downtown to the river. To stop the forbidding blank walls of new buildings and their dehumanizing effect on the streetscape, new structures were required to have shops or cafés at street level. Historic preservation was advanced. A gregarious, intensely social architecture and form of city planning emerged. The friendlier new urban face was enhanced by excellence in new streetscape and building design plus an imaginative, sometimes whimsical outpouring of public art on the streets of the city.
- The downtown is lively again at night and so popular that the new light rail system initially carried more passengers into the city on Saturdays than on weekdays.

## *Catalysts for Change*

The prospects for downtown Portland were not altogether bright toward the end of the 1960s and at the start of the 1970s. There had been spurts of fresh construction—a Hilton Hotel twenty-three

***Bucking the national trend, downtown Portland increased its retail market share with the help of a regional light rail system opened in 1986.***
*(Photograph courtesy of the Tri-County Metropolitan Transportation District of Oregon)*

stories high, a Georgia Pacific structure soaring 375 feet, a 536-foot bank building ominously described by its architect's press agent as rising "40 stories into the air, a towering challenge to Mt. Hood." However, critics were noting that virtually all these megastructures, with their blank walls and dull corporate entrances, lacked sophistication and created such fantastic parking demand that stretches of the city were being turned over to parking lots and garages. At the same time, there were serious concerns about air pollution along the Willamette corridor.

Retailers were worried that a major chunk of their business was being lost to the Lloyd Center, the city's first major shopping mall, about a mile from downtown on the east side of the Willamette. Shoppers were getting weary of fighting downtown parking problems. The number of downtown housing units plummeted from 28,000 in 1950 to 11,000 in 1972. People freely talked about the center city as "a wreck." "We're definitely under the gun here. Many downtown blocks have become ugly parking lots or disused old buildings," a department store executive told a visiting reporter from Seattle (David Brewster, "Sweeping Downtown Plan Unites Portland," *Argus,* March 3, 1972).

Political discontent was building, too. Terry Shrunk, a decent but not terribly imaginative man, had been mayor for more than a decade. There had been little turnover among the five elected "commissioners" who doubled as city council members and executives of specific departments of the city government. In 1969, a young legal aid service attorney, Neil Goldschmidt, told us he considered Portland's entire city government old and out of touch with real problems (interview with Neal R. Peirce, July 2, 1969). There was no substantive effort, he complained, to "humanize" redevelopment plans or stem an alarming decline of public transit caused by suburban commuters' indifference to the center city.

By 1970, however, the chain of longevity among Portland's commissioners was broken as death and retirement opened the way for the election of three aggressive young commissioners—Goldschmidt among them. In 1972, he swept to election as mayor and moved immediately to elevate both professional city planning and neighborhood voices to a much more prominent role than they had ever before enjoyed. He shifted the focus—but exploited the powers—of the Portland Development Commission, created by Mayor Shrunk in the late 1950s, to push forward aggressive urban renewal projects.

It was a classic case of conflict between "old" and "new" forms of reviving troubled cities. Mayor Shrunk and the people he put in charge of the Downtown Commission represented the strong prodevelopment voices of the time—business interests that proved themselves quite ready, in the name of progress, to bulldoze and "renew" marginal neighborhoods on the fringe of downtown. They also tended to be strong backers of continued superroad construction.

Goldschmidt, by contrast, worried about urban renewal projects that "devastated the inner city." He developed a strategy to wed downtown promotion, protection of neighborhoods, and the advancement of public transit rather than superhighways. As Portland State University Professor Carl Abbot would later observe:

> Goldschmidt shared the ideas about the value of density and variety in healthy neighborhoods that Jane Jacobs articulated in *The Death and Life of Great American Cities.* He hoped to use improved public transit not only to reduce air pollution along the Willamette corridor but also to serve well-preserved everyday neighborhoods, and to focus activity on the downtown. A vital business center would protect property values in surrounding districts and increase their attractiveness for residential investment. Neighborhood planning would focus on housing rehabilitation and

on visible amenities to restore confidence in older residential areas and make them competitive with the suburbs.

(In *Portland: Planning, Politics, and Growth in a Twentieth-Century City.* Lincoln: University of Nebraska Press, 1983.)

It would prove to be a brilliant political strategy, a vital backdrop to the 1972 Downtown Plan, but the plan itself was not originated by Goldschmidt. Indeed, most of the critical events preceded his election. Of these, the most critical had to do with a parking garage.

For two decades, Meier and Frank, one of downtown Portland's major retail anchors, had owned a two-story parking garage in the block diagonally across from their store. The structure, operated by Union Oil, was painted gold and blue and ranked among the Northwest's ugliest urban structures. Then, in 1971, a Tacoma, Washington, developer approached Meier and Frank suggesting construction of a twelve-story parking structure on the site. The department store executives, anxious to kick their way out of sales doldrums, thought it was a great idea. (Explanation of one of the civic leaders of the era: "All retailers want parking within one block of the hosiery counter—that's their conception of how far a woman will walk.") Meier and Frank went public with the new garage proposal, seeking city approval, and all hell broke loose.

The problem was that the site, the block running between Sixth and Broadway, Morrison and Yamhill, was not just any old downtown block. The parcel was purchased in 1849 by shoemaker Elijah Hill for $24 and a pair of boots. In 1858, it became the site of the first public school in Oregon. In 1883, the Northern Pacific Terminal Company purchased the block for $75,000 as the site for a new hotel. The Portland Hotel, a $1 million Victorian extravagance designed by Stanford White, opened in 1891. For sixty years, its verandas, ballrooms, and restaurants would be the center of Portland's downtown life. During the hotel's glory days, virtually every president of the United States stayed there once.

In 1951, though, succumbing to the so-called business wisdom of the day, the grand old hotel was razed and replaced by the two-story parking garage. Loss of the hotel generated public outrage. People began to talk of reclaiming the block as a public square. Thus, when Meier and Frank came forward with its idea of a twelve-story parking skyscraper, citizen reaction was instant—and negative. The city's planning commission found citizens carrying antigarage signs at its hearing. The city council decided the political price was too high, and the garage was a dead letter.

Rebuffed on the garage, Meier and Frank and its business

friends approached Mayor Shrunk to ask for a comprehensive parking plan for the downtown, but as they got into dialogue with the professionals at city hall, they soon learned the problems of the downtown's future ranged far more broadly than where cars were to be parked.

Some elements of Portland business were well primed for a debate on downtown issues. With Richard Ivey of the engineering/urban planning firm of CH2M playing a key role, the idea of a "Downtown Plan" was advanced and a committee of some twelve top business leaders formed into a so-called Portland Improvement Committee. The group, in short order, tapped the business chieftains for $110,000 for a study. (The critical fund-raising meeting was held at the First National Bank boardroom, with a key executive from Georgia Pacific going around the table extracting money from the assembled executives. "Some didn't know why they were there; they found out in a hurry," Ivey recalls.)

The city and business group recruited Robert Baldwin, the widely admired planner for Multnomah County, to head the effort, and got Rod O'Hiser, one of the city's senior planners, along with Carl Buttke, another transportation planning consultant, to work with the CH2M consulting team. The velocity of this effort and its close ties to city hall raised concern in some quarters, however. A number of vocal citizens, including civically concerned architects and neighborhood activists, expressed alarm about business interests' dominant role. They worried that major planning for the city's future might go forward with minimal public involvement.

In response to those concerns, Mayor Shrunk—at Baldwin's urging—decided to appoint a broadly based citizens committee. As its chair, he designated Dean Gisvold, a young lawyer who just happened to be a supporter of the mayor's sometimes rival—liberal city commissioner Neil Goldschmidt.

The Citizens Advisory Committee (CAC), which then took form, was a far cry from your standard blue-ribbon committee to address some city problem. Among its seventeen members were representatives from the general public, from business, and from environmental and arts groups. It divided itself up into subcommittees on such topics as transportation and parking, housing, retailing, and the future of the city's waterfront—and then let any citizen of Portland join any one of those subcommittees. Gisvold recalls:

> The first thing we did was set up a range of meetings, downtown and in the neighborhoods, to see what people would like the downtown to be like. We went to Southwest, to Northeast Portland, all over the city, with at least one meeting in every neighborhood. All our meetings were well publicized in advance. We got *The Oregonian* to run a questionnaire we

devised. We held six meetings downtown for workers there too. We talked to 1,000 or more people. We maintained close communication with a proliferation of groups that sprang up in response to the planning process, such as Citizens for a Car-free Inner City, Save the Forecourt Fountain, and a group promoting electric transit. As a result of this dynamic grassroots process, a community's attention was focused on a fading downtown, and a commitment made to revitalizing it. It seemed that everyone was interested and excited, including the media.

Over the course of fourteen months of intensive activity, the CAC worked closely with the professional planning team to frame the city's Downtown Plan goals and guidelines. A project office was opened downtown, a kind of "neutral turf" neither the territory of city hall or the business interests. "It was a nice ground-floor space downtown with a tree coming out of a pot and through the roof," Ivey remembers. "People could come in and were welcomed to bring in their ideas."

Through this highly collaborative process, with every camp from the major businesses to city hall to architects and neighborhood voices intimately involved, a far-ranging plan evolved. The process was so inclusive that virtually every group could claim some part of the authorship. In contrast to traditional, highly prescriptive master plans, the initial document was basic and "doable," not highly detailed. In fact, such basic longer term issues as light rail were not addressed at all because they did not seem reachable during the early stages of plan development.

The plan focused less on specific solutions than general guidelines for approaching each issue area. It went through a seven-month approval process. First the City Planning Commission worked it over, and then, just before Goldschmidt became mayor in 1972, the city council approved the plan with remarkably little dissent. The council members were in fact relieved to receive a plan on which the major players had already reached such broad consensus.

## *Accessing Downtown*

Portland during the late 1960s and late 1970s was experiencing grave air pollution problems—indeed, its air was so dirty it violated federal standards one of every three days. It was becoming overwhelmingly clear that any automobile-first solution to downtown Portland's access problems would be gravely flawed.

Yet any approach centered on *restricting* access to the downtown would have encountered near-frantic opposition from business and its allies. Public transit thus emerged as the compellingly logical alternative. The Downtown Plan came down resoundingly in its favor and for the restriction of single-person auto use.

Subsequently, a major contribution was made by a review panel headed by Betty Merten, a long-standing citizen activist working closely with such figures as Ron Buel, Goldschmidt's chief assistant. They were involved with STOP (Sensible Transportation Options for People), which was lobbying for transit and for the defeat of the Mount Hood Freeway. Building on the 1972 plan's recommendations, these activists were able to reconceptualize the problem from one of *parking* to one of *access*. They also exchanged the rhetoric of controlled growth (as a way to achieve cleaner air) to a focus on controlled means of access.

Two inefficient private bus firms had been providing transit to the city and its suburbs—a situation remedied in 1969 by the Oregon Legislature's creation of the public Tri-County Metropolitan Transportation District. Tri-Met *did* improve downtown's bus service. Critical problems remained, though—chiefly, how to provide efficient bus service when private autos competed so vigorously for available road space. The answer that emerged was the transit mall, a major north-south couplet (Fifth and Sixth avenues) devoted almost exclusively to buses. (The city council visited Minneapolis, viewed the Nicollet Mall there, but decided ultimately for the two streets in the belief they would make a much more forceful statement for transit, as well as impacting twice the property that a single malled street would.)

As critical as the *whether* of a transit mall was the *how*. The eleven-block-long mall stretch was devoted primarily to bus use. Portlanders found themselves treated to widened sidewalks paved in handsome brick with granite curbs, fountains, benches, historical light standards, public art, and special glass and bronze bus shelters. Big sycamores and London Plane trees were selected to give a special Northwest feeling to the scene.

The transit mall's art was robust, depicting Northwest themes as common as rain and indigenous animals. Norman Taylor's Nordic nude, *Kvinneakt*, evoked particular notice. (*Kvinneakt* later won national notoriety when a poster was published showing a man, from behind, spreading open his raincoat in the statue's direction with the poster title "Expose Yourself to Art." The human posing in the poster, Bud Clark, was at the time proprietor of Portland's Goose Hollow Inn; he would later become mayor of Portland.) Roger Shiels, whose firm was retained by the city and Tri-Met to direct the mall's architectural/design/engineering components, recalls that procurement officers at UMTA (the federal Urban Mass Transportation Administration) were extraordinarily nervous about letting some of

***Along the eleven-block transit mall, Portlanders are treated to wide sidewalks of handsome brick. Sycamores and London Planes add the Northwest touch.*** *(Photograph courtesy of the Tri-County Metropolitan Transportation District of Oregon)*

the federal grant monies go for the art on the Portland mall. "They agonized for months over it. I finally went back to Washington and said I'll stay here until you approve it. As it turned out, I only had to wait three or four days."

UMTA paid, in fact, 80 percent of the Portland transit mall's $15 million costs. For its money, the federal agency got not only excellent design but some notable innovations in mass transit. The mall emerged with the world's first closed-circuit television system to provide riders at each of the thirty-one stops with around-the-clock arrival and departure information plus route information to any part of the three-county Tri-Met service area. A second television system, at eight locations on the mall, permitted riders to punch a particular route number and see locations and times of buses along the route. A third part of the information system provided a series of color-coded photographs to identify the seven geographic areas covered by Tri-Met.

There was a degree of political risk associated with the mall: for two years, right up to his 1976 reelection campaign, Goldschmidt had to explain a torn-up downtown. (He was reelected easily anyway.) Nor did the mall's physical plan work out entirely smoothly. As Shiels acknowledged a decade after the opening: "Some of the ceramic pieces had to be taken away. With the very heavy use, the whole project now needs restoration. Buses have incredible wheel loads and beat up the street badly. Granite has had its problems. Design-wise, it's been a very controversial project."

Public acceptance of the mall, however, was high at the start and remained that way. With the addition of the light rail connection in 1986, downtown transit ridership achieved a cumulative *50 percent increase* over fifteen years. By one estimate, if those downtown trips had not been served by transit, nine forty-story garages would have been needed to accommodate an equal number of trips. As it was, the total number of downtown parking spots scarcely changed.

***Norman Taylor's Nordic nude,* Kvinneakt, *evokes particular notice. Federal Urban Mass Transportation Administration funds helped bring art to the mall.***
*(Photograph courtesy of Rodney O'Hiser, Portland, Oregon)*

Though the 1972 plan did not specifically mention light rail, the Metropolitan Area Express (MAX) system was a logical outgrowth—and, needless to say, a key Goldschmidt project. Its roots lay in controversy over the proposed eastside Mount Hood Freeway (named for its view, not its destination). Funded with interstate highway monies, the road would have benefited suburban commuters while eliminating 1 percent of Portland's housing stock and diverting substantial traffic to neighborhood streets.

Predictably enough, the Mount Hood Freeway proposal gave birth to a strong Portland antifreeway revolt. Goldschmidt took up the fight against the road as soon as he became mayor and through a long series of maneuvers eventually won the support of Republican Governor Tom McCall, an avid conservationist, and, just as critical, the state's powerful Transportation Commission chairman, Glenn Jackson. The Mount Hood Freeway project was withdrawn, most of the scheduled federal matching funds ($85.7 million) diverted to the light rail system. (On repeated occasions, requisite political and budgetary support for the trade-in of the interstate segments for the light rail system appeared to be in serious jeopardy. One of the critical clearances was made by President Jimmy Carter's Secretary of Transportation just before Ronald Reagan assumed the presidency and put most major transit projects on ice. That cabinet secretary was none other than Neil Goldschmidt, who had left Portland in 1979 to accept the cabinet post for the last phase of the Carter administration. Later, Goldschmidt returned to Oregon, serving as governor from 1987 through 1990.)

The fifteen miles of the MAX system were planned to connect downtown Portland with the suburban city of Gresham, fifteen miles to the east. For downtown, the decision was made to put MAX's tracks at street level. Like the transit mall, brick sidewalks, trees, attractive street furniture, fountains, and art were included, but the decoration was more muted. Most of the "stations" were simple curbside stops, marked by a series of coordinated brick pavers. (The cobblestones used, according to Shiels, were ships' ballast from times past.) Nothing more obtrusive than a dark stone block separated the transit loop from an adjacent vehicle lane, yet however "simple" the design approach, MAX gained instant and continued ridership support.

By the late 1980s, yet another Portland transit innovation was being planned: vintage trolleys to run at nonpeak hours on the light rail tracks. The trolleys, connecting the downtown shopping district with the new Oregon Convention Center and Lloyd Center on the opposite (east) side of the Willamette, underscored a growing Portland concern to connect, in tangible ways, the interests and activities of both the west and east sides of Portland. The ritzier west side, with the downtown proper, most of Portland's vast parklands, and several handsome residential sections, had perennially seemed favored. The east side was the scene of more industry and a great polyglot of neighborhoods, ranging from poor black to wealthy white Protestant to a number of Catholic communities (including a flourishing beer-drinking pub culture). The city fathers' clear intent was to achieve more balance by awarding the east side such desirable facilities as a convention center, following a coliseum and federal office buildings sited there earlier.

The trolley project was the brainchild of a group of business leaders headed by Bill Naito, a remarkable Japanese-American and entrepreneur/civic leader whose role reminds one again of how it is people, not official programs and bureaucracies, that propel a city forward. Starting in the 1960s, Naito, sometimes with the assistance of his brother Sam, took the lead in repeated investments and innovations to make downtown Portland strong and resilient. He purchased and rehabilitated numerous buildings in the Skidmore/Old Town District, helping transform that downtown neighborhood from "skid row" to a community of restored nineteenth-century elegance with safe streets, fine shops, and some of Portland's best restaurants. While most of downtown was in the doldrums, Naito also swam against the tide to purchase the dilapidated 1920s vintage Rhodes Department Store on a key downtown corner. He removed the center sections of each floor to take advantage of the building's skylight, filled the building with small shops and restaurants, renamed the whole "The Galleria," and proclaimed it America's "first vertical atrium shopping center."

As if all that were not enough, Naito in the 1970s got control of a chunk of riverfront close by the center city, put in 302 units at his McCormick Pier Apartments, and popularized the idea of middle-class downtown living. He was also a chief backer of Art Quake—Portland's annual downtown outdoor festival; any important Portland civic board seemed to feature a Naito family member.

Every statistic seems to affirm that the increased access to Portland's downtown, the goal so fervidly sought by business leaders and the citizen planners of the early 1970s, has happened, that the system is working. Total downtown retail space has risen to five million square feet, including 120,000 in Naito's Galleria. Two new department stores have opened, including the much sought after Nordstrom chain. Construction began in the late 1980s on what boosters predicted would be the most important project in the history of downtown—Pioneer Place, a major four-block project, with a value set at more than $100 million, being developed by the nationally known Rouse Company. The first phase was to include a 280,000-square-foot office tower, a 60,000-square-foot Saks Fifth Avenue department store, and 174,000 square feet of specialty retail.

Not every project has succeeded. The Yamhill Marketplace, a festival market financed in part with city and federal Urban Development Block Grant moneys, opened with much fanfare in 1982 but was in receivership by 1989. City officials hoped positive spillover from Pioneer Place's one hundred shops, opening nearby, would be enough to stem the red ink.

## *Pioneer Courthouse Square*

It was a sure bet that the 1972 Downtown Plan would mirror Portlanders' opposition to anything even faintly resembling the parking high-rise that Meier and Frank had planned for the historic Sixth and Broadway site; and so it was. The plan endorsed open space development of the block, saying this should be Portland's "central space," dedicated neither to commerce nor governance. It set in motion the lengthy negotiations necessary for the city to purchase the block.

It would take years, though—another twelve, to be exact—for the ultimate solution, a grand public space known as Pioneer Courthouse Square, to emerge. Up to the end of the 1970s, attention focused on the city's new transit mall. Finally, in 1980, the Portland Development Commission announced an international design competition. No less than 162 design entries were received. The jury's ultimate choice was the proposal of an interdisciplinary team, headed by Portland architect Willard Martin, for a great brick plaza that people could get to easily from surrounding streets and buildings. It would be an intensely open, public space.

The concept of the piazza, the grand public space, is far more European than American, and it was an idea that did not, initially, sit well with downtown businesses. With all that exposure and lack of security, said many, all manner of undesirable "types" would be attracted to Portland and to its very heart. Architect Martin said the square would become the "living room for the city"; businesses feared the living room might be socially repelling. Frank Ivancie, a politician close to the business crowd, became Portland's mayor and in January 1981 declared Pioneer Square dead.

There followed yet another public outcry. A citizens' fund-raising committee, Friends of Pioneer Square, went to work to convince the city to keep the project moving. This proved a strong grass-roots movement. The committee stumbled onto a gimmick that turned out to be a brilliant idea—selling personalized bricks at $15 a piece. Some two hundred volunteers were involved in selling bricks in person and on the phone and mailing share certificates. (No other city had tried this idea before; afterward, a number of cities, New Orleans included, would copy it.) The Friends group also launched a major gifts drive, "selling" such architectural features of the square as columns, drinking fountains, trees, trash receptacles, and grates. In all, some $1.5 million was raised. It was enough to convince city hall, which then began to commit public funds, commence construction, and appoint a nonprofit organization to manage and operate the public square. More individual bricks were sold—eventually more than 60,000.

Finally, on April 6, 1984, the 107th anniversary of the opening of the Portland Hotel, Pioneer Courthouse Square was officially dedicated. Residents streamed in to discover a vast central space—one that William H. Whyte, America's foremost advocate of sensitively planned center cities, pronounced to be the largest urban downtown space to have been built in the United States in many years. Yet, added Whyte,

> the important thing is not the size. Nothing is more unifying for a city than a lively central square where the city can come together. The creation of this new one sets an example that cities everywhere should heed.

Within the square were large and small amphitheaters, a bronze and glass pavilion with a "bistro-style" restaurant, an open-air market, a lectern for public addresses, a monumental colonnade, a dramatic fountain, and an enclosed lower level housing retail shops and Tri-Met's customer assistance office. From the past, there was a special reminder: the wrought-iron gate of the Portland Hotel, placed precisely where it had originally stood.

Supporters noted that Portland was bucking a prevalent urban development theme of the 1980s—cities allowing the erection, at their very hearts, of mammoth private structures walling off street life. (One example is architect John Portman's massive hotel complex on New York City's Times Square.) Instead, Portland seemed to be rededicating itself to its role as a street town. On its central square, the most valuable piece of real estate in Oregon, it had replaced a parking garage with a place for the city's people.

Whimsically, socially, politically, at lunch, and on grand occasions, Portlanders have since made Pioneer Courthouse Square their common space.

The square's yearly operational funding of some $200,000 also reflected the public-private partnerships that have evolved in "post-Plan" Portland. Some 35 percent of the $200,000 came from city grants, 40 percent from rents paid by the restaurant, bookstore, and vendor carts on the site, 15 percent from commercial establishments in the nearby downtown, and 10 percent from special fund-raising events. Virtually none of this richness was explicit in the original plan; it was negotiated as the plan evolved over the years.

## Waterfront Park and the Design Ethic

As critical as any element in the 1972 plan—and Portland's eventual image to the outside world—has been the expansive Tom McCall Waterfront Park. Bordering downtown, it was appropriately enough named for the governor who led two great battles—one for the cleanup of pollution along the entire Willamette River and a second for creating a park at this location.

A high-speed waterfront roadway had, as in too many cities, placed a roaring concrete artery between Portland and its waterfront. There were even proposals to broaden Harbor Drive, as it was called, to ten lanes.

Again, alert Portlanders objected and demanded this part of their city inheritance be returned to them in the form of a park. The 1972 plan took their side, and McCall, Oregon's governor from 1967 through 1974, happily signed onto the park crusade and pushed it over the qualms and objections of highway engineers who predicted monumental traffic tie-ups if Harbor Drive were closed down. As it turned out, alternative traffic routes were available and there was scarcely a ripple when Harbor Drive passed into oblivion.

In its place, Portlanders got a handsome park, bordering the downtown's buildings on one side, the river on the other, with winding paths, fishing piers, and, in recent years, twinkling strings of white lights strung along the bridge superstructures. It is yet another of Portland's distinctive *people* places, as well as a site for a variety of city festivals.

A spirited competition emerged for the rights to develop a big chunk of waterfront land directly south of the park. On one side was the Naito brothers' development firm, on the other Cornerstone Development, a Seattle, Washington, firm owned 80 percent by Weyerhaeuser and run by Paul Schell, a former candidate for the mayor of Seattle. It was a happy circumstance in which the city was likely to do well, whichever side won. Cornerstone was eventually selected and built a handsome complex, "RiverPlace," which features a waterfront esplanade, including the Alexis Hotel, 190 up-

***In 1958, getting access to the Portland waterfront was no picnic.*** *(Photograph courtesy of the Oregon Historical Society, O.H. 57776)*

***When Harbor Drive was transformed into a park, monumental traffic tie-ups never materialized.*** *(Photograph courtesy of the Oregon Historical Society, O.H. 87453)*

scale condominum units, an athletic club, and a floating restaurant and two hundred–boat marina (constructed by the Portland Development Commission).

The waterfront's handsome appearance is no exception in today's downtown Portland. Looking for reasons, one could say that the appearance of quality, of cleanliness, and of orderliness stems from controls imposed by the city's official Design Review process. (Chief among these are the bans on forbidding blank walls and the carefully negotiated rules on stepped height limitations as the city slopes down toward the river.) However, there is so much else. The city's plethora of fountains and greenery adds to the pleasant image. The public art adds a quality of sheer delight—you can touch the beaver, rub the seals' noses, play with the fountains. (The public art is not so esoteric as to require a college education to appreciate what one is seeing—all the pieces can, in fact, be read at several levels.)

Historic preservation, grievously ignored through the 1960s when many valuable buildings were lost, now flourishes in Portland

***Rubbing a seal's nose is an irresistible tradition. Much of the transit mall's art depicts Northwest themes.*** *(Photograph courtesy of Rodney O'Hiser, Portland, Oregon)*

and enhances the scene materially. Rehabilitation has focused, appropriately, on the Yamhill and Skidmore/Old Town historic districts, which encompass the largest assemblage of Victorian cast-iron building facades east of the Mississippi. Some forty downtown historic structures have been rehabilitated, at a cost of some $125 million. Among them are the 1869-era Pioneer Courthouse, across the street from Pioneer Courthouse Square.

Some new buildings of real distinction have also risen in recent years. Among them is the 1983 Justice Building, the most humanized court and jail buildings we have seen in any major city anywhere. Among the Justice Building's features are hanging basket copper light fixtures and reflected glass windows designed by Edward Carpenter and, on the sixteenth floor, the Portland Police Museum, designed to look like an old-fashioned police precinct house. The structure practically everyone truly notices, though, is the Portland Building (1982), designed by Michael Graves as one of the nation's first postmodern structures. With its beige, blue, and maroon tiles, the Graves design has variously been called electric, imaginative, precedent-shattering—and an oversized jukebox. Outside is Raymond Kaskey's thirty-five-foot-high *Portlandia* statue, trident in hand. It is said to be the largest hammered copper sculpture since the Statue of Liberty. Ten thousand Portlanders lined the river and streets to watch *Portlandia*'s triumphant trip to her pedestal. Author Tom Wolfe chose to call the happening "the greatest public art event in the last 90 years."

Portland is not only a pretty city, it is a clean and welcoming one. For visitors accustomed to the typical banes of the latter-day American cityscape—street filth, overbearing design, and occasional surliness—Portland offers a magical antidote. Easterners liken Portland to a Disney set, all clean, all perfectly polite, and they are not altogether wrong. Downtown merchants even hire their own Disney-like "helpful people" to walk the streets answering questions, reporting problems, and assisting those in need. These young folks, in green uniforms, get training in "friendness" at a local community college. They are intended to reassure shoppers and to be a quick helping hand if someone has a sudden health problem, is victimized by a pickpocket, or gets badgered by rambunctious teenagers.

To please the eye, Portland offers not only public art (1 percent on all city projects since 1980) but scenes anyone anywhere would have to enjoy. A handsome Chinatown Gate and Dragon were constructed in the 1980s, for example, and there are hanging flowers on the cast-iron street lamps of the historic districts. To please the ear and eye alike, there is the two-block-long Portland Center for the

Performing Arts, home of the Oregon Symphony Orchestra and two theaters.

"Promote downtown as the entertainment and cultural center of the metropolitan area," urged the 1972 plan. The counsel has clearly been followed.

## *Housing*

Portland is not simply a happy Disney stage set. It is also a real, gritty city with its share of such deep social problems as domestic violence, drug and alcohol abuse, and even gang activity spreading up the West Coast. It is a city in which low-income housing units have oftentimes seemed an endangered species. The 1972 plan addressed the decline in downtown housing stock as well as the flight of the middle class from downtown and called for a one-for-one replacement of low-income housing units removed from development projects. With foresight, the plan also called for new middle- and upper-income units in downtown to help provide a base for a true twenty-four-hour-a-day inner city.

The housing goals have been tough to fulfill—especially on the lower income side. By 1980, the city faced a serious decline of housing for the poor. The League of Women Voters conducted a thorough survey and reported many old apartment buildings were closing down due to fire and building code violations and that the downtown business community, exerting pressure to expand, was tempting owners of old hotels and apartment buildings to sell out for a profit. In a follow-up study nine years later, the league found the loss of low-income housing downtown was continuing, exacerbating the problem of homelessness, the new ingredient in the housing crisis. By the mid-1980s, in fact, some two thousand to three thousand Portlanders, many of them alcoholic or mentally disturbed men, were roaming the streets. Rare was the night that every one of the 114 cots at the emergency night shelter were not occupied.

The league in 1989 also reported that actual housing abandonment was increasing, the problem compounded in some neighborhoods by the infiltration of drug dealers and gangs "who occupy the vacant houses, degrading and terrifying whole neighborhoods." Despite the 1972 plan's goal to protect downtown's stock of low-income housing, the actual count of rooms in SROs (single-room occupancy hotels—downtown's only significant source of housing for the poor) fell by 59 percent, from 4,128 in 1970 to 1,702 in 1986.

Portland's social services advocacy group, Central City Concerns (CCC; formerly the Burnside Consortium), became particularly vocal in urging creative response to the growing homelessness issue. It insisted that *permanent* low-income housing was needed, that a shelter was *not* a home. CCC itself began in the late 1970s to buy up imperiled buildings, especially SROs. By 1988, it was administering 737 units, with hundreds more soon to come on-line. Step into the lobby of such establishments as the Estate, the Palace, the Rich, or the Broadway—some seventy or more years old—and you meet kindly but worldly-wise managers trying to provide the SROs' gnarled residents with a better alternative to the street. In the words of Ron Van Rheen, a Portland SRO manager: "We do lots of parenting. Wake tenants up for doctors' appointments, give a hand with their mental health problems. But we have rules, too—live by them or we'll refuse to rent to you." In fact, what Portland has accomplished is a kind of hierarchy of SROs, from the emergency shelter up to beautifully painted and maintained facilities. Kick the booze and drugs and rowdiness, says Van Rheen, and "you earn your stripes to move up."

There is also a downtown shelter for battered women, and Dean Gisvold, the head of CCC, told us that the loss of SROs had virtually halted and that clear city commitment had emerged to keep all that are left. A good amount of old warehouse space was also being converted to lower cost housing.

A thorny question remained: How vigorously should a city seek to free its downtown of panhandlers, "street people," the mentally disturbed, and others who may scare off potential downtown customers? Portland retailers have complained, on occasion bitterly, of the city's tolerance for "alternative" life-styles.

At least on the homeless front, there has been a major effort to reach accommodation. In 1987, CCC and downtown merchants/property owners agreed to put a lid on shelter beds that might attract more vagrants even while endorsing strong efforts to preserve surviving SRO units and thus stem the growth of homelessness. A downtown housing preservation agreement, reached a year later, committed the city's major players to a serious effort to eliminate the need for mass shelters by the end of 1991, mainly through creating five hundred new units of housing for the homeless and very poor. The Portland Development Commission agreed to select and develop sites, the Portland Housing Authority to secure operating subsidies, CCC to own and manage the new buildings, and the Portland Metropolitan Chamber of Commerce to raise funds for case management for individuals aimed at breaking the cycle of homelessness.

The most interesting member of the partnership, in one respect, was the Portland Development Commission (PDC). Begun by

Mayor Shrunk, the commission's chair for several years was Ira C. Keller, the respected civic leader who would later have one of Portland's splendid downtown fountains named after him. He was also the Portland leader historian Carl Abbott likened to New York's Robert Moses "in his willingness to use appointive office and personal prestige to impose his own vision on a changing city." It was under Keller's leadership that the PDC, in the 1960s, carried out the aggressive clearance of the so-called "South Auditorium" area on the southern edge of downtown.

The PDC's executive director of the time, John Kenward, called South Auditorium a "blighted and economically isolated neighborhood" deserving demolition to make way for offices and business services and perhaps an inner loop freeway. Aside from bulldozing many acres, the project had two important results. It convinced many Portland business leaders that the PDC and the city had real business acumen—and thus could be trusted to carry out many of the ambitious projects endorsed in the 1972 plan—but it also frightened Portland's neighborhoods, setting the political stage for Neil Goldschmidt and what would become one of the nation's most neighborhood-sensitive city administrations.

The PDC's bulldozer-oriented leadership could not have welcomed Goldschmidt's election as mayor. His allies had actually been prime movers of a Portland City Club recommendation calling for the agency's abolition, but Goldschmidt decided to co-opt, not extinguish, the PDC, and with fresh appointments the agency was ready to do his bidding. In successive years, the PDC became a highly effective team player on every front, from design competition for Pioneer Courthouse Square to guiding the construction of innumerable public projects. It provides a model other cities might consider: an agency to test the feasibility of potential city projects (applying "reality checks"), to assemble financing (industrial revenue bonds, tax increment financing, and so on), to actually letting out construction contracts. A five-member agency appointed by the mayor and confirmed by the city council, the agency seems to have learned how to apply the test of public interest and need, to work with the rest of city government in setting the public agenda *before* it engages developers to carry out a project.

Withal, Portland old-timers had to chuckle when the bulldozer urban renewal agency of yesteryear was committing itself by the late 1980s to a partnership agreement aimed to building hundreds of housing units for the poorest of Portland's poor.

As for the 1972 plan's pledge of a full range of housing, the RiverPlace project added a reasonable quota of luxury condos. The Naitos' McCormick Place addressed the upper edge of middle income, and from the 1970s provision was made for some two thousand units of lower middle income housing close to Portland State University, directly in the downtown area. The city continued to set goals of increased middle-income housing to add vitality to the downtown and prevent competition by middle-income households for lower cost units.

## *Tying It All Up*

What led to the 1972 Downtown Plan's long-term success?

The fabric has multiple strands.

First, a remarkable consensus was achieved among sometimes warring camps—major corporations and neighborhoods, developers and environmentalists, small businesses and social activists. The consensus reflected, to be sure, the potential for mutual respect and accord inherent in Portland's history and civic culture. It was a process marked, some of the participants told us eighteen years later, by "patience and modest persistence, creeping incrementalism rather than revolutionary moves." In the words of architect-planner Gregory Baldwin:

> The downtown "Portland Story" demonstrates a means by which desired public and private urban development can be stimulated without restrictive or prescriptive regulations and without strong economic incentives. It tends to illustrate that if one neighbor can be shown it is in his interest to complement his neighbor's interest, he will do so, and in the process confirm that a good urban environment is a natural state, and should be pursued accordingly.

Indeed, while most American cities of the 1970s and 1980s saw developers become the driving force, putting forth their proposals, then barely tolerating public input, Portland evolved the idea that *the public's agenda* comes first. The process tried to accommodate the interests of the poor, but its leitmotiv was the downtown as everyone's place and the critical necessity to lure the middle class, indeed the very affluent too, back into the heart of the city. In an age of increasing privatization, with people drawing back into the shells of their private cars and private fenced-in houses, Portland's 1972 Downtown Plan represented a critical *return to public life,* underscored by investments in such places as Pioneer Courthouse Square, the bus mall, and Waterfront Park. In the long run, the Portland approach also turned out to be an extraordinarily healthy one for private business interests.

Second, there was the incredible effort put into entertaining all viewpoints and ideas: consider that the leadership of the Citizens Advisory Committee (CAC) had to take a community list of some one thousand ideas, reduce that list to some three hundred things to do, and then refine the list to some one hundred truly manageable in scope and character.

Third, the spirit of inclusiveness, of keeping everyone informed, became ingrained and helped maintain support for the plan. "We try to involve lots of people with complementary interests," a chief player told us, suggesting that Portland is a city where getting everyone on board leads to action, not the civic paralysis it might cause in many cities. The CAC, so key in preparation of the 1972 plan, was actually continued for the first phase of the Goldschmidt administration, providing reviews of major downtown projects and facing showdowns with developers on a couple of occasions. After two years, Goldschmidt apparently decided the political costs were too high and decided not to reappoint the CAC's members to new terms. After CAC's demise, Goldschmidt typically appointed ad hoc citizen-business consultative groups to oversee individual projects, such as the transit mall and Pioneer Courthouse Square. Observers noted it was a procedure that gave him more control plus an opportunity to take personal credit.

Born of the 1972 plan, a neighborhood alert system flourished and remained active. Even in the late 1980s, we heard, the city had a list of ninety-three neighborhoods to be regularly informed of developments that might affect them. Some 116 businesses and 100 different environmental groups were also on the alert system. As any student of urban affairs can attest, early "warning" systems, keeping all camps informed, can avert a huge portion of potential standoffs.

A fourth factor in the plan's success was Portland's remarkably clean politics. Kickbacks, payoffs, and sweetheart deals are so rare that suspicion of them does not paralyze (or discredit) the system. "This is an honest place. Intelligence is sometimes at issue, but not integrity," a leading figure in the 1972 plan's implementation told us.

Fifth, the plan enjoyed excellent political prospects because its salient principles—to assure a vibrant downtown, promote public transportation, and assure housing and further neighborliness—fit like a glove the agenda of incoming Mayor Goldschmidt in 1972. By the time he left office in 1979, they had become articles of faith in Portland's civic culture.

Sixth, the plan came forward when Oregon's great twentieth-century environmentalist governor—Tom McCall—was in office and ready to assist. Oregon's nationally pacesetting land-use plan, enacted under McCall and successfully defended by McCall against hostile initiatives all the way to the last months of his life in 1982, set an ideal context for the 1972 plan and its implementation. The first principle of the state plan was participation and the idea that regions should evolve their own development plans, set their own urban growth boundaries, and stick to them. The state plan's central principle—to maintain the vitality of urban centers and to keep cities from sprawling out onto agricultural and timber lands—provided an expansive context, and one could say ongoing validity, to Portland's efforts.

Finally, Portland's 1972 Downtown Plan succeeded because it was relevant, because it addressed, in creative fashion, pressing problems of the time, from air quality and transit to downtown employment to saving the waterfront for the people, problems that Portland could not afford to ignore.

When Portland felt ready in the mid-1980s to move a step farther, to a Central City Plan to encompass a broader area than the downtown initiative of the prior decade, the 1972 plan was neither ignored nor rejected. Quite the contrary, it was consciously built on and proclaimed the basis for the next steps. Critics said the Central City Plan lacked the same drama and fervor of its 1972 predecessor. Some went so far as to suggest the city had become more bureaucratic, more ossified in its operating procedures over fifteen or so years; but in methodology and goals, the Central City Plan echoed 1972 almost point by point. As Commissioner Earl Blumenauer told us in 1988:

> The citizen-based and citizen-driven planning process took over three years, involved a 15-member steering committee and about 150 members of eight functioning advisory committees. . . . The effort epitomizes Portland's philosophy of planning for the future rather than waiting for breakdown and failure to get the community's attention.

Shades of 1972! Blumenauer continued to outline highlights of the Central City Plan:

> The plan focuses on the Willamette River, using it as a unifying element rather than a barrier dividing the "east" and "west" sides.
>
> The plan requires 5,000 new housing units within the central city. . . . We've opted to make housing mandatory as well as provide tax incentives, subsidized loans and zoning bonuses.
>
> The plan limits height and floor area ratios (bulk) in order to preserve Portland's human scale of development. . . . It protects views for the public and protects Pioneer Courthouse Square and the Forecourt Fountain from shadows that would be cast if tall buildings were built adjacent. . . . Less development means that we will have more projects on more blocks and more construction jobs. This plan is an alternative to the philosophy

of some cities, supported by some elements of our business community: bigger projects and taller buildings.

Mass transit continues to be emphasized with the plan calling for construction of an additional light rail corridor to the west.

Reading the Central City Plan in 1988, one indeed had the feeling that the 1972 Downtown Plan had become institutionalized, had become Portland's new conventional wisdom. Yet the fact remained: Portland's basic tenets, 1972 and 1988 versions alike, constituted a revolution in city planning, city building, and city social relations. It was a revolution still waiting its dawn in most cities of America.

## *Commentary: Portland*

GEORGE E. HARTMAN, JR.: It is terribly difficult to define excellence in architecture and urbanism. If I have to create excellence in architecture, I can't get much done, but there is a very effective way for even the public to begin to achieve better architecture and better urbanism. That is through the process of choice: "I don't know what a good building is but if you give me two buildings, I can quickly figure out which one is better." People may not know what they want but they can make choices.

This chapter begins with a crisis of choice: the loss of traditional commercial markets to the fast-growing suburbs. That's a choice. You can decide if you'd rather have those markets downtown or in the suburbs. You can make that decision.

Portland faced a clear-cut choice when the city tore down a hotel and replaced it with a two-story parking garage. One could quickly look at that and say: "I would rather have the hotel. The hotel is a better building for this site." Faced with those alternatives, it's easy for people to figure out what they want to have happen. The choice process was at work throughout this Portland project. Abstract choices about urban excellence can't be tackled but the real choices are easy to work with.

ROBERT SHIBLEY: That's a lovely way to frame the idea of how crisis generates change for the better, how that energy gets transformed. The choices—suburban versus downtown, hotel versus parking, highway versus waterfront park, large-mass buildings all the way to the waterfront versus the step-down aesthetic—all of these were presented to the public in the form of simple dichotomies.

I think there's a trap in this conception. With hindsight, we can identify a few apparently key decisions, but we can also appreciate the incrementalism of this plan. A set of principles was put in place that then got tested one building or project at a time. The dichotomies, your system of choices, don't give you the unity and cohesiveness that a plan needs. The strategic plan implementation that we saw in Portland came from a set of principles. Framing the whole process in terms of a series of dichotomies doesn't necessarily give you a good downtown.

There were some principles driving choice in Portland. We are going to step down to the waterfront. We are not going to let a highway separate us from our waterfront. We are going to maintain our block size—one of Portland's great gifts—and so on. These were principles with strong physical implications. The plan took a position that was then negotiated and argued about over specific buildings. A very sophisticated academic debate took place.

What I love about the Portland plan is that those principles were so immediate to that city, that region, that set of political and social circumstances. The principles govern how you translate from the choice environment and put a single building into context. You may derive some of these principles from examining available choices, but then the principles kick in and start to take over.

HARTMAN: The decision to limit heights and floor areas to preserve Portland's human scale of development again reflected a simple choice: "Would you rather have a few large projects or many small ones?" People chose many small ones. They argued that less mass development meant more projects on more blocks and more jobs. I would add that smaller projects are also more likely than large projects to be appropriately designed because they are easier to manage, and smaller projects are easier for people to evaluate. The choices become sharper.

SHIBLEY: Part of the success of this project derived from the primary placement of public perception and public good. As it happened, that priority turned out in favor of the business community. This is really dramatic, especially in light of the piecemeal growth that you've outlined. It meant that many small, local developers could play a role and play in a way that the money stayed in the area. It was a "grow-your-own-developer" plan as well as a physical proposal.

HARTMAN: The primacy of the public agenda was established very early on, but initially there was a battle between the people and the planners and architects. In general, the decision-making process has been abandoned to professionals during the twentieth century. In

Portland, you had the people and the politicians who represent them wresting the decision-making process back from incompetent and indifferent professionals who were not working in the public interest.

**SHIBLEY:** I think it's more complicated. The initial short-term business interests and the traditional solutions to business problems had been driving Portland to its demise prior to 1972. One example was the notion that the location of the hosiery counter tells you where to put the next parking garage—one block away. This was a straightforward business demand, but it should not be the wisdom that drives decisions on downtown access.

The choice process helped citizens and the business community to coalesce. Portland was "blessed" early on with some of the grand-scale urban renewal projects of the mid-sixties. The citizens said, "We don't want another large-footprint, homogeneous development that tears up the fabric of the city."

**HARTMAN:** The business interest is really quite simple. They don't really care where the hosiery counter is or where the parking is. What they want to do is increase sales and profits. They start looking at pieces of the problem in order to do that and their first move is always to put the parking closer to the shopping.

**SHIBLEY:** But what happened in Portland was interesting. The business interests who were unhappy with their inability to get their customers close enough to the hosiery counter took charge of the planning process. Only then did the citizens, architects, and planners put in enough checks and balances relative to this business initiative to organize a plan.

I am worried about thinking of this as a linear process, as "Let the citizens set their agenda, then bring in the planners." The process in Portland over the last twenty years was one where the architects and planners were brought in early, working hard with the public to frame those choices.

**HARTMAN:** There is a parallel between architects and planners and the military. Most urban decisions are too important to be left to anybody's notion of personal gain or political expediency. People have to be in there, deciding how they want this thing to come out. When you get the planners aligned with the public goals, as in Portland, they are effective at implementing them.

The people's interests and the business interests are not necessarily at odds, but they are both often at odds with the planners' interests. Planners are trying to implement a theoretical agenda. The planners' notions often are out of touch with the public. They mean to do things to save society but society is perfectly capable of saving itself. When the public decides on its goals, then the planners and architects can be brought in to implement them.

**SHIBLEY:** Oregon's culture is important here. It's a culture of participation and public involvement. The first tenet of the state land-use planning process demands a very clear community articulation process. There's a tradition of citizen advisory committees in Portland and a strong belief in a planning process that is structured that way.

**HARTMAN:** Three underlying elements made this project work. The first was the primacy of the public agenda and second was the necessity of inclusiveness. The third thing the citizens, planners, and politicians did was to maintain continuing accountability. The fact that nobody quit, that the people didn't lose interest, and that the government didn't abandon them means that everyone remained accountable.

The primacy of the public agenda means that the big issues—what we are going to do rather than how—are matters everyone is involved in deciding from the very beginning. The public, not the professionals, should decide *what* is to be done. Then the professionals can help decide *how* it is to be done. They are much better able to design the stuff than set the policy. That way you also get public support for designs that are responsive to the goals. You cannot have the medical profession deciding who is going to live. When we decide who will live, then the medical profession is ideally situated to implement that decision.

**SHIBLEY:** There are some issues here of equity and diversity. A fair amount was made in the press about Portland's comeback: that it was a victory, in their rhetoric, "for all the people." In reality, it was a reclamation for the middle class.

One needs a fairly exclusive income level to be able to take full advantage of Portland's downtown. The original intent of the plan was for housing replacement as development occurred: one-for-one replacement; but this was "one-for-one" beginning in 1972, when the city had already lost a large amount of its downtown housing and its lower income housing in particular. These issues have not been addressed in the way that was hoped for in the original planning document. This is evident now in some of the problems in North Portland and other areas.

**HARTMAN:** It does seem that it was set up with a middle-class bias, but that was probably the right way to do it. The upper class will take care of itself. One needs to take care of the homeless. By focusing this project the way they did, the sponsors were able to co-opt the support of the largest number of people, and that seems smart.

**SHIBLEY:** That might be all right strategically, but some subtler things give one pause. The project has been referred to as a kind of Disneyland set. Folks in green uniforms are being helpful to tourists and visitors but they also are helping the homeless out of the area. Given the grit, vitality, and diversity that one looks for in a healthy, vibrant city, the sense of homogeneity about downtown Portland, both in its physical design and in the population it serves, takes the edge off an otherwise incredible success story.

**HARTMAN:** Of course there is less diversity in Portland. One of the things that makes this project easier to do in Portland than in Washington, D.C., or New York City is that the city is a more homogeneous, more cohesive place.

**SHIBLEY:** It's more cohesive in two ways. The rivers, the topography, and the short blocks all tend to make it "work" as a city. It's imageable, understandable. It has that physical advantage. And, in general, Oregon doesn't have the history of diversity. It didn't have the immigrant experience of the East Coast or Seattle or San Francisco, but it's a myth that Portland is homogeneous. The reality is that it has had a fair influx of Asians and blacks.

The lip service was that this was a downtown plan for everybody. That rhetoric was necessary to make this project successful, but I question whether it is true. A certain part of the life downtown is less for that failure. It feels less real and more Disneyland stage set because that diversity is lacking.

Also, I'm hearing a fourth principle evolving in this conversation. Add diversity to primacy, inclusiveness, and accountability.

**HARTMAN:** Diversity is right. Areas of urban excellence often come from local diversity and larger, common goals. The pieces often represent very personal things that need to be based locally, but they can work together to make the town or state or country work. Diversity is not incompatible with a larger unity.

**SHIBLEY:** There need to be places where everyone across the ethnic mix can be together at the same time that there are ethnic enclaves with a strong physical and social character. That may not be working yet in Portland.

HARTMAN: It also may be misleading to say that such a project can be done without government support on a large scale. The Graves building with the *Portlandia* figure is a massive piece of urban subsidy. It's completely occupied by government workers. When you take large buildings like this to complete a project, it's done with quite a bit more subsidy than you think. I don't think that's bad. That's what the government should be doing to further this project.

SHIBLEY: Much of the product of a huge project like this is the process itself, which continues to interrogate it and develop it over time. It's never done.

CHAPTER 3

# Boston's Southwest Corridor: People Power Makes History

Viewed from the lofty reaches of the Prudential Center, fifty stories above the crowded streets of Boston, the city spreads northward to the horizon and the New Hampshire mountains peaking through distant haze. The patrician stone and brick mansions of the Back Bay continue for blocks, forming a clean, orderly grid that looks as though it was lifted intact from a drafting table. The emerald green Esplanade runs along the Charles River, which itself is dotted with teams out for crew practice and sailboats. Beyond the Charles River stand Harvard University, the Massachusetts Institute of Technology (MIT), and Cambridge. To the east, past the steely blue reflecting presence of the John Hancock Building and the downtown skyline, the North End juts into the murky gray water of Boston Harbor. Across the harbor, planes taking off and landing at Logan Airport are stacked in the sky as far as the eye can see.

The precincts of the ordinary Bostonian spread north, south, and west. Closeby, Fenway Park sits adjacent to the Back Bay Fens, one of the grand spaces created in the nineteenth century as part of Boston's "Emerald Necklace" of parkland. The South End, with block after block of brick row houses, continues for a mile and then blends into low-slung, mostly poor Roxbury and its red-brick public housing projects and wide, empty spaces. Beyond Roxbury lies the hilly greenery of densely packed, working-class Jamaica Plain, one of Boston's biggest neighborhoods.

From fifty stories up, the Southwest Corridor looks like a spine of greenery curving through the cityscape in a five-mile-long path, out from Back Bay and the downtown, out toward the suburbs. Or-

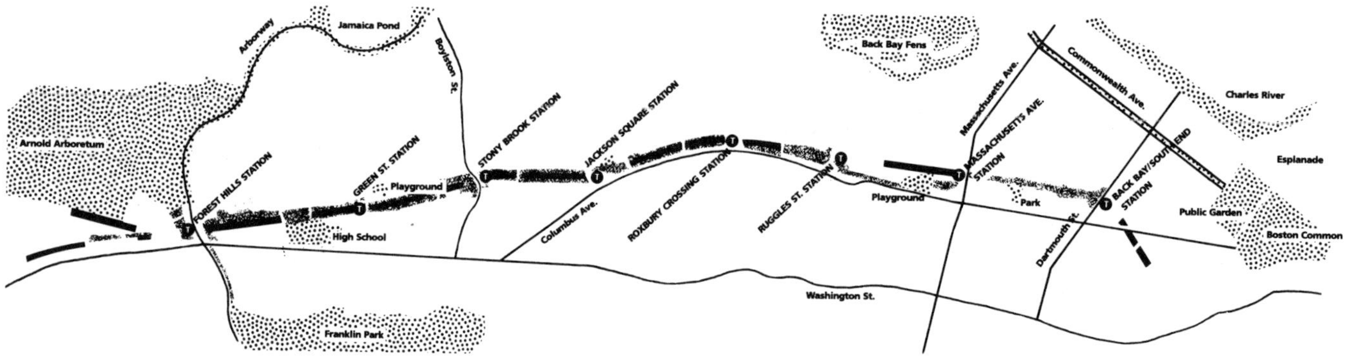


***A map of the fifty-two-acre "linear" Corridor Park.***

*(Drawing courtesy of* Places, A Quarterly Journal of Environmental Design)

ange subway cars looking like brightly painted toy trains from a distance run up and down tracks through the corridor. Bridges criss-cross the tracks. Walking and bicycle paths dart in and out of greenery.

At the ground level, standing in the small red-brick plaza that serves as the entrance to Corridor Park in the South End, details obscured by altitude come into focus. Teenagers shoot hoops at a basketball court alongside an apartment building. Neighborhood residents—young and old, black and white—stroll through the park. Students lugging backpacks filled with books wander by on a path planted with trees and bushes, mixing with lawyers toting shiny leather briefcases. Kids moving a little too fast for the territory zoom by on neon-bright skateboards, jockeying for position with bicycle riders. Children play in a nearby playground, and further along an older woman works in a vegetable garden. An occasional car slowly moves down an adjacent street deliberately designed with curves and bends to discourage traffic. The incessant sound of construction noise emanates from nearby buildings, structures wrapped liked gifts in plastic tarps to keep the weather out and construction debris in. Town houses are being renovated. Some new office towers are taking shape behind them. A rumble gradually builds in the distance, becoming clearer and more resonant as a train thunders through the tunnel underfoot.

Come sunset, the streetlights in Corridor Park flicker to life. Floodlights throw soft light onto the marble and granite of Copley Place, a ritzy complex of shops, restaurants, and two forty-story hotels, complete with an outpost of Neiman-Marcus. Across Dartmouth Street, which always buzzes with the flow of traffic, the huge neon sculpture at the Back Bay subway and train station bathes both the sidewalk and passing pedestrians in warm, glowing tones of red, yellow, and blue. The activity in the park, which functions as a huge backyard for thousands of neighbors, does not skip a beat. A couple sits hugging and kissing on a bench, with the electronic sounds of dance music blaring out of a boom box decorated with yellow happy face stickers, emblems of the late 1980s and early 1990s resurrected from the 1960s.

Life along the Southwest Corridor. Day and night. Winter and summer. Work and play. Beginning as a narrow park shoehorned into the crowded South End, the corridor's long skein of parks, playgrounds, basketball courts, gardens, and recreational areas becomes wider as it curves across Boston, one of the most attractive, inviting ribbons of greenery in urban America. In the park, kids play ball. Underground, commuters read their papers on the way to work. Beneath this oasis, under concrete decking in the South End, lies the Massachusetts Bay Transportation Authority's relocated Orange Line subway, plus commuter rail and Amtrak lines serving the busy Northeast Corridor.

Thanks to the careful community planning and sensitive urban design that went into building it, the Southwest Corridor thrives precisely because it has a split personality. Even for Boston, a city with entire neighborhoods such as Back Bay reclaimed from the water in the nineteenth century, the corridor project stands out as one of a kind. It was the biggest public works project in Massachusetts's history and one of the most ambitious planning, design, and construction jobs—with one of the largest casts of characters—ever undertaken in any American city.

It took more than two decades, and nearly $750 million, to get the job done. When work began, the area was an inner-city wasteland, an ugly no-man's-land overrun with ailanthus that had been created in a rush to clear the way for a new interstate "inner belt" highway to the suburbs. The highway never came, thanks to the

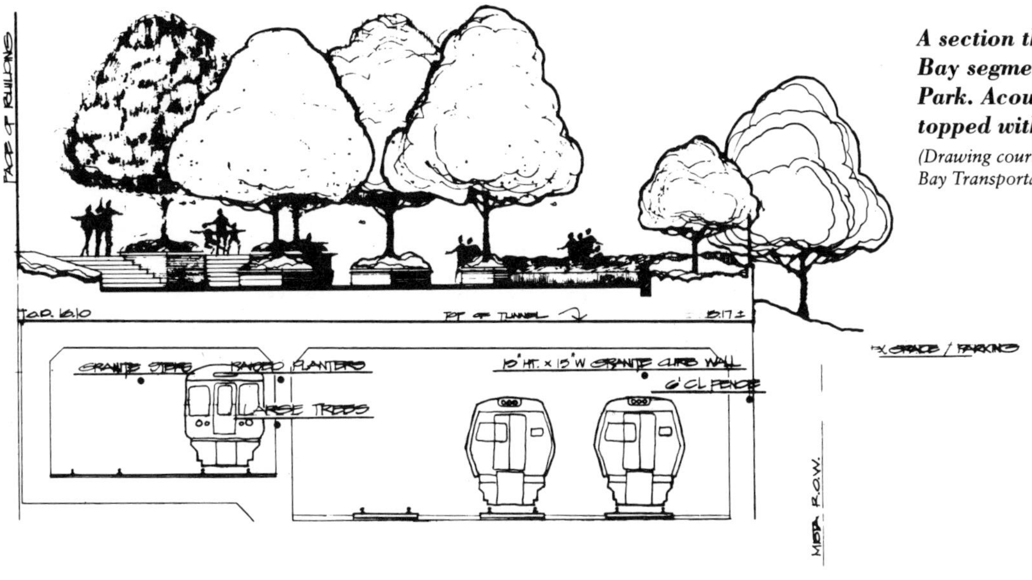


***A section through the Back Bay segment of Corridor Park. Acoustic decks are topped with landscaping.***
*(Drawing courtesy of the Massachusetts Bay Transportation Authority)*

Bostonians—poor, middle-class, wealthy, black, white, and Hispanic—who flexed their political muscles and eventually killed the plans to build the road. However, the damage had already been done by bulldozers and wrecking balls. The long gash cleared for the highway curved out from downtown, up to a half mile wide in some places, roughly paralleling the course of the Penn Central Railroad's tracks to New York City. It looked as though someone wielding a giant machete had gouged out the city's heart.

The corridor had never been an attractive place. The railroad tracks had been there since early in the nineteenth century, cutting through Boston atop a high granite embankment that cut off neighborhoods and severed access across the city. Clearing land for the aborted highway only made matters worse, but when planners, designers, builders, and ordinary residents were finished, the park they created had become the biggest addition to Boston's open space inventory since landscape architect Frederick Law Olmsted transformed the swampy, malodorous "Fens" into green space. In places, Corridor Park runs above the subway and rail lines. In other areas, it continues along both sides. All told, there are fifty-two acres of parkland, twenty playgrounds, sixteen basketball, street hockey, and tennis courts, and ninety community gardens. Moreover, there are nine architecturally unique subway stations (some doubling as stops for commuter and Amtrak trains), twenty-six new bridges across the corridor, a huge new storm drainage conduit for a thirteen-square-mile area, a community college in Roxbury with thousands of students, two high schools, five hundred units of housing, and other development projects.

It takes just fifteen minutes on the Orange Line subway to travel the Southwest Corridor in its entirety from the Back Bay station to the end of the line in Forest Hills, but along the way the rider—or better still, the walker, jogger, or bicyclist—gets to sample integral parts of Boston the average visitor rarely sees. This is not the Boston of historic Revolutionary War monuments and historical sites or the picture postcard streets of well-heeled Beacon Hill. This is the heart and soul of the city, gritty and workaday, in all its rough beauty and glory.

As it wends its way through the city, the corridor skirts nearly one-third of Boston's people and traverses seven distinct neighborhoods. The journey begins in the South End, a 1990s melting pot neighborhood of old and new, rich and poor. The neighborhood did not even exist until a huge landfill project in the late nineteenth century created dry land out of underwater tidal mud flats. Today, the South End is a neighborhood of attractive Victorian brick row houses and walk-up apartment buildings lining quiet side streets. It is one of Boston's most diverse neighborhoods, a mixture of whites, blacks, Latinos, Asians, Arabs, and dozens of other ethnic groups. Along the South End's edges are some of the most recognizable skyscrapers on the Boston skyline—the Prudential Center and the John Hancock Building—plus the Christian Science complex and Symphony Hall. To stroll down Columbus Avenue, the main street of the South End a couple of blocks from Corridor Park, is to walk through a curious mixture of the upscale—with expensive gourmet food shops, boutiques, and galleries—and the old—butcher shops open since the early 1900s, unpretentious eateries, and pawn shops.

Little was spared to design and build Corridor Park in the South End. A mile of concrete decking was built to cover the transit corridor, creating a narrow park that has won plaudits from urban designers and landscape architects. Where trains once roared on open tracks, noise levels are now equivalent to normal street noise. Ventilation stacks to clear smoke from the tunnels were ingeniously designed so that they would appear to be avant-garde additions to existing red-brick row houses. They blend into the landscape so well that one scarcely notices them unless they are pointed out.

***Where trains once roared on open tracks, noise levels are now equivalent to normal street noise.*** *(Photograph courtesy of Peter Wrenn, Jamaica Plain, Massachusetts)*

At Ruggles Street in the heart of Roxbury, a giant cantilevered steel and glass station rises from empty land, beckoning as the neighborhood's new "front door." At night, the station comes alive with light, a beacon in drab surroundings. Roxbury is one of Boston's oldest neighborhoods, settled in 1630 on solid land by the British. Today it is the heart of black and Hispanic Boston and also Boston's poorest neighborhood. Along Columbus Avenue, which becomes part of Roxbury as it exits the South End, signs of inner-city commerce are everywhere. "Money exchanges," those inner-city substitutes for banks with big signs proclaiming "Checks Cashed," dot the street. Other placards and posters fill in more details: "Save Money." "Roach Killer." "Christ Died for Our Sins." "Mandela" is a reference to the black-led movement in Roxbury to secede from Boston and form the independent city of Mandela, not some memorial to the South African antiapartheid leader.

Traveling the mile and a half of the Southwest Corridor in Roxbury, one gets a snapshot of what the neighborhood was, what the demolition for the highway left in its wake, and glimpses of what it might someday become if promises to rebuild are kept. As Columbus Avenue leaves the old, dense heart of the neighborhood, it passes through sobering territory. Along the way are four grim, large public housing projects. Some of the buildings fit the depressing stereotype of public housing. The structures are boarded up, surrounded by weeds and trash, and covered with forbidding graffiti. Some buildings are neat and well-maintained, though. Part of the Bromley-Heath public housing project, they have been taken over by tenants, who now run and maintain them.

In Forest Hills, the busiest of all the stations at the southwestern terminus of the Orange Line, about two miles distant from Roxbury, a metallic white modernistic clock tower climbs from the station, a new landmark in the neighborhood. Near the station, community residents are out cleaning the park. Garden plots mark its boundaries. Children bounce up and down on a teeter-totter in a new playground a few blocks away. Nearby are the Arnold Arboretum and Franklin Park, two huge expanses of greenery linked by Corridor Park.

This is Jamaica Plain, part of Boston since 1874, nestled between Roxbury and the independent town of Brookline. It is a venerable neighborhood of tightly packed wood-frame houses dotted with the empty hulks of local breweries that used to be a main industry. Jamaica Plain still shows the marks of its domination by the breweries—block upon block of homes built by the brewing companies for their employees. There are only a few feet between buildings, and their designs are as identical as the boxy little houses in any prefab suburban subdivision. Many of the homes in Jamaica Plain are what the locals call "triple deckers," modest, three-story Victorians often shared by two families.

Hilly and with a tangle of narrow, twisting streets, Jamaica Plain has long been an Irish stronghold in Boston, though its northern reaches experienced a large influx of blacks and Hispanics during the 1960s and 1970s. Along some streets, red-brick "fixer uppers" have been restored by the neighborhood's increasing community of young professionals attracted by the relatively low housing costs. On some little side streets, such as Mozart Street, however, Jamaica Plain's poverty is obvious. The buildings have seen better days. Paint is peeling. Garbage is everywhere. A few wrecked cars sit at the curb. Large knots of Hispanic kids occupy street corners. Viewed from the top of a nearby hill, the skyline of downtown Boston with its imposing skyscrapers can look like a mirage.

Any visitor to the Southwest Corridor in the early 1990s had to admire its vitality. The park was heavily used. The transit line was a success, providing fast and clean transportation to some 50,000 riders every day. Yet the Southwest Corridor remained very much a work in progress, a project whose outcome was still in doubt. Huge parcels of vacant land still sat beckoning on the corridor's periphery. In Roxbury, idle land often seemed to stretch as far as the eye could see, awaiting the promised development of shops and more housing to replace what bulldozers leveled.

Immediately east of the busy Roxbury Ruggles Street station sat a five-and-a-half-acre parcel of land begging for redevelopment, land known locally as Parcel 18. The stark expanse, kept neatly mowed and free of trash, was a symbol of both the hopes for the future of the Southwest Corridor and for progress that appeared to be a long way off. A local task force was still meeting in 1990 trying to figure out just what to do with the land, which planners had foreseen as a new center of shops, offices, and hotels. Many residents were visibly angry that the promised development and jobs had not materialized. They suggested that their neighborhood was being left behind as the rest of the corridor thrived.

The original plan described Roxbury's future in the kind of glowing, flowery verbiage that planners are wont to write: The Ruggles Street station, the plan said, would

> embrace a major new mixed use urban center. It will include extensive retail, residential and institutional space, as well as limited office development totalling 500,000 to 750,000 square feet. It also offers the first opportunity in years for a new hotel and entertainment center in Roxbury.

In some ways, the Southwest Corridor plan was typical of its species. It was too boring, too long, and in places too hard to follow. Yet it was also unique since many planning documents bear only a slight resemblance to the final product. Not infrequently, they sit on a shelf and gather dust—but not along the Southwest Corridor. Anyone who looked could see quite concrete ways that the plans had materialized. There was only one major failure: Roxbury. The plans had focused most heavily on economic development in Roxbury, but little of the promise had been fulfilled. An attempt in 1988 by then Governor Michael Dukakis to get a state agency to relocate to Parcel 18 as its anchor tenant was rebuffed when the agency declined to move to the inner-city site.

Along Washington Street, another one of those urban commercial strips with shops offering cheap, bargain goods to customers with limited incomes, the old El tracks had been torn down and the sun shined on sidewalks that had sat in the shade for most of this century. The girders that used to support the elevated tracks poked out of the sidewalk or the middle of the street like amputated limbs. The old Dudley Street station, an elevated monstrosity that served as a major transfer point, sat rotting. "Replacement service" was supposed to come to Washington Street as soon as the old Orange Line was torn down, inasmuch as the Southwest Corridor is a brisk fifteen- to twenty-minute walk away. Yet "replacement service" was slow to materialize. The neighborhood, city, and transit authority continued arguing about what constituted replacement service, and many Roxbury residents missed the convenience of the old El service. In Jamaica Plain, where a trolley line was taken out of service, some residents were still trying to get the old trolley service restored.

Anthony Pangaro—the man who oversaw much of the Southwest Corridor's planning in the 1970s—called this the project's "unfinished business," elements of the project no one expected to be resolved immediately. As Massachusetts entered a money squeeze even tighter than the one it struggled through in the 1970s, however, prospects for an early solution to the corridor project's unfinished business, the needs of Boston neighborhoods most desperately in need of redevelopment, appeared dimmer than ever.

## *The Rise and Fall and Rise of the Southwest Corridor*

Back in 1948, a warm public response awaited the Master Highway Plan for eastern Massachusetts with its recommendation of building Interstate 95 (I-95) through Boston. The plan seemed to be a matter of keeping up with the Joneses. The late 1940s were the dawn of the national race to build highways, and Boston would not be a laggard. It would have a new eight-lane, elevated highway linking downtown with the loop highway around the city (Route 128, Massachusetts's famed high-tech development corridor). The plans seemed reasonable enough. No one could foresee the forty years of conflict the highway would engender.

The original plans actually envisioned a network of highways to carry thousands of cars daily through Cambridge as well as densely populated southwest Boston. More than 90 percent of the bill was supposed to be footed by the federal government, which was freely dispensing money for interstate highways. In the late 1950s and early 1960s, Massachusetts started acquiring land for the highway by eminent domain. By the late 1960s, the state Department of Public Works was relocating families and demolishing homes and businesses that stood in its path.

Yet as the public taking continued, public outcry was also intensifying about the extent of demolition, the loss of homes and businesses, the negative impact of the empty land, and threats to neighborhood stability. Real physical devastation undermined some neighborhoods. The specter of the roadway and demolition looming in the near future threatened others. Anger mounted along with community action aimed at stopping the highway. Concern spread to areas outside the city, such as Cambridge, where many politically influential residents felt threatened by a roadway network that was eventually supposed to pass hard on their community too. Recalls Pangaro:

> It was the dawn of the environmental era and the urban antihighway people found a common ground with the suburban environmental people. There were a lot of people in Cambridge for whom the example in Roxbury was very vivid. They saw black people's homes in Roxbury and white people's homes in Jamaica Plain getting tumbled. They didn't want it to happen there.

The highway project, as it turned out, died long before the state government turned to taking and clearing land in Cambridge, but not before antihighway political fervor had hit a high pitch. Bostonians and suburbanites—far removed from each other not only by location but also by ethnic origins and economics—joined in groups such as "Save Our City," "Operation Stop," and the "Coalition to Stop I-95." The latter eventually became the Southwest Corridor Land Development Coalition, the major community force in redeveloping the cleared land.

Land in the corridor was cleared to make way for the highway in the late 1960s. The roadway was not officially abandoned, however, until 1972 on the heels of public protest and a change in the political winds that had favored urban highway building. Left to await some new use, the corridor became a desolate trail of emptiness from Back Bay and the South End out to Roxbury and Jamaica Plain. Decay and arson began along the edges of the Southwest Corridor and fanned outward like a rash, although the extent of damage varied according to neighborhood.

In the South End, minimal demolition for the highway took place. Open railroad tracks continued to separate Back Bay to the north from the South End on the other side of the tracks as they had for more than one hundred years. With each passing train, the neighborhood shook and a plume of blue diesel smoke settled over the local streets. Uncertainty over whether a superhighway would replace the railroad tracks led to the neglect of property and serious disinvestment.

Roxbury bore the brunt of the damage. There, a corridor of man-made devastation took shape as acres of land on both sides of the railroad tracks were cleared to make way for the planned eight-lane, elevated highway. More than sixty-two acres were cleared in Roxbury for a section of highway that was supposed to be less than 1.5 miles long. More than three hundred businesses fell to the wrecking ball, taking more than two thousand jobs from the neighborhood. Some nine hundred families lost their homes. The landscape in the vicinity of the highway corridor was ruined.

More land was cleared and more homes and businesses were felled in Jamaica Plain, the neighborhood that was to become one of the key battlegrounds in the long fight to stop the highway and repair the damage from wholesale land clearance. In Jamaica Plain, the harbingers of urban decay—trash-strewn lots and boarded-up and burned-out homes—radiated from the empty corridor land.

The state had moved to clear property in Jamaica Plain and Roxbury with unusual dispatch. About 110 acres of land had been emptied for the roadway by 1969; plans for even more clearance were alive and well. In Roxbury alone, another one thousand people were living under immediate threat of displacement by the highway, even as the opposition coalesced. In both neighborhoods, servicemen coming home from Vietnam found the solid communities where they had grown up bearing a sad resemblance in places to the Southeast Asian country they had just left behind. The battle cry became "Stop I-95. People Before Highways."

Ellen Anderson, who was an aide to Pangaro during the rebuilding period and was in college when the first buildings were leveled to make way for the planned highway, described the devastation and the protest this way:

> The thing I remember about the Southwest Corridor was coming up to the old railroad underpasses and seeing all of the "People Before Highways" graffiti. In Cambridge you saw signs saying "Cambridge Is a City Not a Highway." I remember taking bike rides and seeing it all. Along Columbus Avenue [in Roxbury] I'd look at all of the buildings that had been torn down and think that it looked like a bomb had hit. It made you sick. Who'd take a community and rip it down like that? Thousands of people were displaced in close-knit neighborhoods. And it was not all done gently.

The eventual death of I-95 was a landmark in public opposition to the type of highway building projects that required the eviction of thousands of people and the clearing of hundreds of acres of land. Responding to the protests in 1970, then Governor Francis Sargent declared a temporary moratorium on highway construction within the confines of the Route 128 outer belt. The bulldozers and earthmoving equipment in southwest Boston fell silent. Meanwhile, Sargent commissioned a regional planning study called the Boston Transportation Planning Review, a $3 million undertaking subsidized mostly by federal money. The exercise was designed to come up with alternatives to the old highway construction strategy. Based on the recommendations of that study, which was conducted with heavy community input, Sargent in 1972 formally cancelled the I-95 routing. In its place, he endorsed relocating the Orange Line, one of four Boston subway lines that, at that time, ran along the elevated tracks through Roxbury. Thanks largely to neighborhood pressure, the substitute plan went well beyond replacing the highway with a subway line. It called for redeveloping all of the land that had been cleared in the corridor, making it available for recreation, for business, and for housing.

Republican Sargent's killing of I-95 may have been warmly received in the neighborhoods that faced even more clearance and decay but his decision was immensely unpopular with the state agencies that would have been charged with building the new highway, with the labor unions representing potential construction workers, and with a variety of local politicians who remained avidly prohighway. In Roxbury itself, opposition came from residents angry about relocating the Orange Line and losing the El service the neighborhood had long enjoyed. Many of the opponents of the recooked plan privately bet the decision would be reversed when Sargent left office in 1974.

Plenty of reasons remained to bet against the plans to rebuild the Southwest Corridor. The construction project would be a logistical nightmare, one involving thousands of citizens and dozens of consulting firms. No model existed to manage a project of such scope, with so many vocal actors and dependent on so many state and city bureaucracies. Designers and administrators alike would have to struggle with the intense political dynamics of a project passing through dense urban neighborhoods. Engineers would have to work in areas with ancient infrastructure and contend with thousands of little obstacles—digging up and replacing ancient wooden water mains, for example. The builders would have to figure out how to do a major construction project in a congested urban area while minimizing the impact on daily life. It was no small task in neighborhoods like the South End, where the construction corridor was a mere one hundred feet wide and the outer walls of many adjacent row houses ended three feet from where the subway tunnel would have to be dug. Another major problem still had to be finessed: the federal money that would be needed to build the new subway line, improve commuter rail service, and build the park was still legally earmarked for building the highway.

"There were a lot of people who felt portions of the highway system should be built because the land was already cleared," Pangaro says. He was Sargent's choice, in 1973, to be the Southwest Corridor's development coordinator, and he became the broker between dozens of competing interests. He recalls:

> The strongest argument for the highway was that the thing was ready to go. You couldn't get the 1,000 houses or the 300 businesses back. The land was a mess. So why not build the highway? The state took a huge gamble on several levels—that they could get the money, that they could figure out what to do with it if they got it, and, finally, that they could organize the project at all.

It would take until 1975 to get the federal money transferred to the rebuilding project and another three years for final approval of the environmental impact statement required to get federal funding, but Boston's timing was fortuitous. There was a rising tide of political resistance to pushing interstate highways through urban areas. Advocates of mass transit were gaining power around the country, particularly in the aftermath of the oil crunch and gasoline lines of the early 1970s. After hard lobbying by the influential Massachusetts congressional delegation, the U.S. Congress made a move that would affect transportation policy for decades to come. It changed the Federal Highway Act in a fashion that permitted transferring the half billion dollars in federal money that had been dedicated to building the highway to the new mass-transit line and park.

The money swap from the Highway Trust Fund to the Urban Mass Transit Administration was, on the surface, a mere bureaucratic reshuffling of government cash, but it was a milestone in federal action, a real policy watershed. The message was clear: No longer would highways be regarded as the premier solution to urban traffic problems. For the first time, a major expressway project had been relegated to the scrap heap and the land and money devoted to other uses. The legislation that enabled Boston to make the switch could also be used by any other state or city that had a change of heart. It was still being used in the early 1990s to transfer money intended to build highways to mass transit instead.

While the scrap over money played out in Washington, D.C., the equally tortuous exercise of writing an environmental impact statement got under way. Hearings on a draft of the voluminous document were held in 1976; the final document was not accepted by the federal government until 1978. Washington officially released $750 million for the transit and park project in 1978, the same year that Ed King, a conservative Democrat who campaigned against the subway project and for the highway, trounced incumbent Michael Dukakis. Once in office, King changed his mind. Construction work on the Southwest Corridor project began in earnest in 1979 and the first passengers rode the new Orange Line in May 1987.

The task of orchestrating the never-ending, three-ring circus fell to Anthony Pangaro and about a dozen associates. Their charge: to run the project office responsible for collecting and refining plans, to build consensus within the bureaucracy and neighborhoods, and to make recommendations to the officials and agencies that had the statutory authority and fiscal responsibility. The office had neither fiscal nor political power. Its only power was the "power" to reach decisions that different state officials would approve. The office was greeted with initial hostility in agencies that were worried about potential transgressions upon their bureaucratic turf, among them the state Department of Public Works, the Massachusetts Bay Transportation Authority (MBTA), and even the Federal Highway Administration.

As a spring snow squall worked on creating a curtain of white partially obscuring the Boston skyline across the water, Pangaro sat in his spacious office on the banks of the Charles River in Cambridge (he had become a real estate developer after his stint on the Southwest Corridor project). Reflecting on the tangled job he was hired to do, and the nebulous authority he was given to do it, he ruminated:

> The state had to do a funny thing. It was going to be responsible for the Southwest Corridor project and it needed someone to pull all these pieces together—streets, transit, city planning, urban design, housing development, and land management. The state owned 120 acres of land, including

> homes, a couple of schools, and a church. People were upset. So they decided to find someone to pull it all together. The only thing was, they didn't give him any real power. The job was cuckoo. On paper it was very loose. It was the power to be persuasive.

Later, as the Southwest Corridor went from planning to design, Pangaro was given formal authority as project manager at the MBTA, the agency charged with constructing the new subway line. The managers of the project were responsible for coordinating fifty-two different firms of architects, engineers, planners, and consultants as they worked with neighborhood residents to determine their needs, to design the subway line and park, and finally to begin the construction project. A small army of consultants came on board, including acoustic experts (hired to quell the noise from the subway and railroad trains), surveyors, geotechnical experts, exterminators (brought in to kill the rats that would be displaced by construction), and aerial photographers. Pangaro left the project in 1980 and construction began under the direction of the transit authority's construction managers.

## *People Power*

Charlie's Sandwich Shoppe on Columbus Avenue in the South End is the kind of place where they have never put Brie on the hamburgers—and never will. The choice is simple: American. It is the kind of place where some of the waitresses still call the customers "hon" and the patrons, who have not taken to the glories of bran muffins and bean sprouts, run the spectrum from construction workers to city workers and lawyers to sweating kids taking five from a game of street hockey. Charlie's Sandwich Shoppe is the kind of place where the fixtures—the old Formica counter and the orange stools for starters—look as if they dated back to the days when Herbert Hoover was in the White House. Some of the mementos, though, like the autographed photo of the New Kids on the Block, the pop music sensation that came out of Boston with a bullet in 1989, are from the era of MTV.

The cramped diner is full of conversation at high volume. The accents are pure Boston. The sound "aaaa-hhhh" wins hands down over "rrr." The sign near the entrance to Charlie's Sandwich Shoppe says it all: "Established 1927. Where Quality and Service Rule." The other sign, hung over the counter packed with people wolfing down burgers and sandwiches with nary a trace of radicchio or arugula but a lot of just-plain-lettuce, says even more: "No Parking After Eating."

Michael Reiskind (occupation: audio-video technician; avocation: community activist) is sitting at a table battling an oversized *Cheeseburger Americanus* with lettuce, tomato, onions, a touch of mayo, and a side of fries. Reiskind moved to Jamaica Plain in 1972, a "newcomer" by the standards of a neighborhood where "old-timers" measure residency by the half century. He is tall, casual, and clearly at home within the crowded confines of Charlie's.

Reiskind's introduction, to what would become more than a decade of work on the fifty-two-acre Southwest Corridor project, came in the form of a flyer dropped off by the postman. He was living in a six-bedroom house he shared with a group of roommates in ethnic, working-class Jamaica Plain, a neighborhood where suspicions ran deep and hostility toward the government after a decade of ruinous bureaucratic meddling was so thick you could cut it with a knife.

Pushing aside his cheeseburger, Reiskind notes:

> These people got burned. Housing was abandoned. Businesses were closed. There was disinvestment. There was arson. The visible lack of people caring was killing the neighborhood. These people had been social science investigated by every college in the area. People would come in and say "I want to help you." Then they'd write their thesis and leave town. Not to mention all of the bureaucratic lying and the broken promises.
>
> I was suspect because I was a newcomer. I was young, living with a bunch of people, unmarried, and didn't grow up in Boston, never mind Jamaica Plain. People tested you. They'd yell at you and see if you backed down and whimpered away. If you passed the tests, slowly, you'd start getting invited to things.

After he was accepted by other neighborhood activists, Reiskind laughs, someone even asked him to run for a state representative's seat from the neighborhood. He eventually gained a seat on the board of directors of the Southwest Corridor Land Development Coalition, the preeminent corridorwide community organization during the planning and construction of the new project.

In Jamaica Plain, hundreds of people like Reiskind painstakingly hashed out even the smallest details of the Southwest Corridor project. There were more than one thousand community meetings. "The courage of the people in the neighborhood was remarkable," he says. "Some people coming to the meetings were in their nineties and knew they were designing a project they wouldn't live to see. Some of them died and never rode it. They came out on snowy nights. If the bureaucrats had half as much courage as the people in the neighborhoods . . ." Reiskind's voice trails off and he doesn't finish the sentence. Traveling the corridor on a sunny day in 1990, pointing out the bright spots in Jamaica Plain and all of the blem-

***Planning for the fifty-two-acre Corridor Park included a thousand community meetings.***
*(Photograph courtesy of Peter Wrenn, Jamaica Plain, Massachusetts)*

ishes that remain to be taken care of, he seemingly could tell a story about every bridge, bench, and hedge in Corridor Park.

Hundreds of other Bostonians who became intimately involved in the corridor project can do the same kind of thing. Planning for the corridor included more than one thousand community meetings to discuss everything from station location and design to the flow of auto traffic, construction materials, landscaping requirements, and use of the adjacent parkland. The huge cast of architects, engineers, and other professionals found that within every mile, and often within each city block, conflicting demands were to be heard. Thousands of residents from the affected neighborhoods were involved with the project, showing up for the frequent meetings and strategy sessions.

From the gritty sidewalks of St. Botolph's Street near the South End, where hookers ply their trade, to the commerical heart of Centre Street in Jamaica Plain, where old Green Line trolleys used to clang to and from downtown, the Southwest Corridor project developed a superstructure requiring a long organizational chart to depict, let alone explain. All told, twenty-five task forces and neighborhood communities took part in the process. The community, of course, was just one layer in the hierarchy of the hundreds of contractors and consultants that worked on the project. Nearly ten years after he left the Southwest Corridor project, Pangaro still remembered the players, the lines of communication, and the responsibility as if he was still on the job.

A joint venture of two engineering firms was selected to coordinate the entire project and watch over systemwide plans and design criteria and station and landscape architecture in the park. The project was divided into three sections—essentially, the South End, Roxbury, and Jamaica Plain. A different set of engineers and architects was responsible for each segment of the project. Each section also had a designated "section planner," charged with keeping up the relationship between the project and the community. Staffers sent mailings and copies of meeting minutes to residents and met frequently with homeowners, business people, and community leaders. Pangaro insisted that all consultants attend the public meetings and moderated many of them. He even had aides conduct "dry runs" before the meetings so that the staff could warn him about potential controversies.

The agreement that was worked out between community leaders and the governor's office, when Pangaro was hired to oversee the project, turned out to be the bible that was used to keep the complicated project on track. Before a word of the environmental impact statement was penned or a spade of dirt turned, the various interests had worked out a "memorandum of understanding" between public officials and local groups active in opposing the highway plans. The agreement mandated that 10 percent of the money for planning and 5 percent of the money for basic design contracts for the corridor be used for community participation and technical assistance. Some twenty local, state, and federal agencies signed on. Pangaro notes:

> There were two principles. One was that we'd look at everything together. And the second was that we wouldn't do anything that we didn't talk to people in these neighborhoods about. The state wouldn't apply for money, the city wouldn't build anything, the park department wouldn't even chop down a tree without airing it at a public meeting. We were trying to fill in the grass-roots side, the part that the government never gets to. Ultimately, most people bought into the project.

The frequent public meetings and hearings called under Pangaro's auspices were open to any and all comers. They operated on a consensus basis: all viewpoints were heard. If consensus emerged, Pangaro was willing to make recommendations on the spot. If there was still disagreement, all of the opinions were forwarded to the transit agency. Engineers, agency staff, designers, and even contractors were required to attend all meetings.

A formal structure allowed residents to have a say in determining the relationship of the new subway line to their neighborhood, including the opportunities for revitalization and redevelopment. Neighborhood committees took part in major engineering decisions, such as the alignment of the corridor, the depth of excavation, and the extent of decking. They also reviewed detailed plans for landscaping, fencing, and graphics. Station area task forces, established for each of the planned new subway stations, kept an eye on station design, development plans, and countless other issues relating to individual stations. Other task forces were set up, on an ad hoc basis, to address individual issues as they arose—everything from reviewing structural canopies designed to cut down the noise from the transit line to trying to get specific parcels of land near the corridor project developed. In the late 1970s, many of the community committees and task forces met nearly on a weekly basis. A few task forces were still meeting in 1990, trying to hash out some of the issues that remained around land development.

The project opened field offices so residents could stop in to learn more about the undertaking. The field offices also distributed the *Corridor News,* a bimonthly tabloid, to more than 10,000 people. The newspaper was distributed at convenience stores, libraries, and transit stops. It was also sent to a mailing list of people who had participated in the project at any point. On top of all that, the project developed a small library of informational handouts to explain any and all possible points about the project, from utility disruption and parking by construction workers to the niceties of rat control. Says Pangaro:

> The biggest problem was convincing people that people from outside the neighborhood weren't going to come in and tell them what to do. We plodded through it. We assured people that we were going to figure out what made sense within their neighborhood. The corridor needed to mend two halves of a neighborhood. So we went about land use planning and determining station location by asking ourselves "What do people on both sides of the project really need?" It turned out to be everything from housing to commercial development. In Roxbury people were ready for large-scale stuff. In other neighborhoods we had old homes to sell off. We simply dealt with each neighborhood separately.

## *What a Determined Band Can Do*

Community participation in the Southwest Corridor was more than an abstract civics textbook exercise. Neighborhood involvement produced results and left an indelible imprint on the project. Residents limited the availability of parking where they felt traffic might be overwhelming. They led architects to design and redesign stations so that the scale and character of the adjacent area would not be threatened. They helped select fences, lighting fixtures, and furniture. They helped control construction procedures so that disruption was kept to a minimum while the new transit corridor was built.

In Jamaica Plain, residents determined where the subway and railroad tracks would be covered over and where they would remain open. In Roxbury, the neighborhood helped select the route of new streets that were built as part of the project. In the South End, community groups negotiated minute details of the project with consultants: how the street ends would meet the park, whether garbage trucks would have enough room to turn around, the height of the curb so that people could not park on the sidewalks any more, the location and design of the ventilation stacks needed for the tunnel.

Community groups such as the Southwest Corridor Community Farm and Boston Urban Gardeners (BUG), a nonprofit established to help poor Bostonians build community gardens, were instrumental in securing land for more than ninety garden plots in the park. They even rescued one thousand old railroad ties and ironwork fencing from the railroad embankment for gardeners to use in landscaping their plots.

For the engineers, accustomed to building projects with little outside input, the entire process became a catechism of sorts. Recalls Robert T. Loney, a soft-spoken senior vice president of Fay, Spofford and Thorndike, the engineering firm that coordinated the entire Southwest Corridor project for the transit authority and designed the South End segment of the project:

> We originally looked at it as just another job, attacking it from the technical viewpoint alone. We were going to go in and do our thing. The more we got involved, the more we realized it wasn't just another subway project. There was more to it and it broadened us. The 1950s' generation of engineers cranked up the bulldozers and went and did the job. This was different. You considered what the effect of everything you did was going to be on the neighborhood. You tried your damnedest to minimize the adverse impact of construction. It wasn't us and them. It was all of us in it together.

Loney laughs when he remembers his first visit to the South End, on the same day his firm won the contract on the project, but it is clearly one of those laughs brought on by the passage of time. Visiting one of the neighborhoods with a colleague, he was confronted

***One of the oases shoehorned into the South End. Community groups negotiated every detail.*** *(Photograph courtesy of Peter Wrenn, Jamaica Plain, Massachusetts)*

by a woman walking a big dog. She was not happy over the prospect of outsiders coming into the community to do a major project. The woman and the dog let him know in no uncertain terms. With a small trace of a grimace and maybe a flash of professional pride, Loney notes:

> In the early days there was a definite hostility toward the engineers. Some people flat-out told me they didn't need some lilly white guy from the suburbs coming in telling them what they'd get. But they found out we'd listen to them, not jam things down their throats. We had open-door policy in the office if anyone wanted to come in.
>
> We got religion. Today there's a growing awareness among my peers that the community does have a say. A lot of us remember the baby carriage in front of the bulldozer that stopped a project. We don't want that. And we won't have it if we take the community along in the process. No surprises. Get them in early. Get their input. Most people realize there's a limit to what can and can't be done in any project. And as long as people are brought in early and kept aware of what is going on it pays incredible dividends.

Residents played a huge role in making sure that security concerns were key in the design of Corridor Park and the new Orange Line—perhaps *the* key issue in ensuring the success of urban parks and mass transit. They helped design the project so that it would be resistant to vandalism, neglect, and tight local budgets that could hurt maintenance and policing. (It was a fortuitous decision considering Massachusetts's precarious finances in the early 1990s, a development that necessitated massive budget cuts and tax increases.) Bicycle paths, for instance, were designed to be wide enough to accommodate police cruisers. Graffiti-resistant construction materials were used wherever possible. Only small trees and shrubs that grew to low height were planted so that security would be easier and there would be no isolated areas removed from public view. Two separate paths—one for pedestrians and another for bicyclers—were created to keep people and bikes apart. Ball courts were clustered around play areas and benches to discourage loitering and keep them under the watch of a variety of residents. In the South End, basketball backboards were actually placed at lower than normal heights in order to preserve the courts for younger children and discourage taller teenagers from using them. In the subway stations, all nooks and crannies where people could hide were eliminated. Pedestrian underpasses were designed so they would be visible in their entirety from fare collection booths.

The touchiest issue arousing neighborhood passions during the planning phase was access across the corridor. Since 1815, the railroad corridor, which ran across an elevated embankment, had divided the neighborhoods. In many areas, the population on one side of the tracks was white, on the other black. Loney recalls:

> In the early days of development people didn't want anyone to be able to come across the corridor. There was real opposition to free access. Everybody wanted access to the park, but they didn't want the people on the "other side" to be able to cross over. As the project developed, people got together at the meetings. They found out that the guy on the other side of the tracks wasn't that bad after all.

In most instances, disputes were resolved by providing access across the park where railroad overpasses permitting access previously existed, but in a few cases, access residents opposed to a free flow of people across the corridor managed to limit access.

In 1981, the citizen participation paid off politically. The project was threatened by an $81 million budget shortfall. The remaining construction cost estimates exceeded the federal government's willingness to pay. Federal officials began ordering the MBTA to cut costs by scrapping escalators, noise canopies, and buying cheaper construction materials, but the community groups proved to be worthwhile adversaries, so well-informed about the project's technical details from the years of meetings that they made convincing arguments to retain most of the elements threatened with the budget ax. (Luck had a hand as well since the budget gap came in the middle of the recession of the early 1980s and the project benefited from low bids submitted by contractors hungry for work.) In a few instances, they even embarrassed federal officials. Neighborhood activists made sure, for instance, to publicize a federal effort to save $20,000 on a $20 million contract by eliminating a special antigraffiti finish on concrete walls. As it turned out, Uncle Sam spent more than $20,000 just administering the paperwork for the proposed change. Says Pangaro:

> The overwhelming lesson is that if you set up a process, commit to following it, follow it, and show people you're following it, there will be results. They may be small things, but they'll be concrete. And when the time comes to make big decisions the support will be there.

## *Tent City*

Sixty seconds. That is the amount of time it takes to walk from the front door of a red-brick apartment complex called Tent City to the entrance of Neiman-Marcus, the retailer famed for its consumer-paradisiacal extravagance. The contrast is too cute, almost cheeky.

***"As the project developed, people . . . found out that the guy on the other side of the tracks wasn't that bad after all."*** *(Photograph courtesy of Peter Wrenn, Jamaica Plain, Massachusetts)*

After all, the library is bulging with stories about urban struggles between the rich and poor. Still, how could anyone familiar with the American city in the 1980s and 1990s avoid the temptation to play with the visual imagery?

In those sixty seconds, a poor Bostonian can stroll from a new clean, modern apartment in Tent City to the cosmetics counter at Neiman's, where a sales clerk wearing a $150 dress and a $75 hairstyle will offer to demonstrate a new facial cream in a six-ounce bottle costing more than the poor person's monthly rent. How did the poor person come to reside in a beautiful apartment with bay windows a short stroll from the woman selling the face cream at Neiman's? That is the crux of Boston's new twist on an old story.

It was 1968, the year inner cities across America exploded in flames in the wake of the assassination of Dr. Martin Luther King, Jr. In Boston's South End, the seeds of activism had already been planted. The War on Poverty was showing chinks in its armor. Boston had laid out an urban renewal plan for the South End in 1964. Four years later, the plan was still going nowhere. Some residents had been evicted from dilapidated buildings, but with each emptied building came more deterioration. Scores of families had already been driven out of the neighborhood.

So neighborhood residents, led by activists who would go on to become prominent in Boston politics in the 1980s, erected "Tent City" on the site of a big parking lot serving downtown office buildings. People used to live on the site—before the buildings were torn down with the promise that new low-income housing would be built to replace them. No housing was forthcoming. The protesters camped out on the parking lot for three days, getting heavy media coverage before many of the demonstrators were forcibly removed and arrested.

"The neighborhood was at the point of exasperation," says Kenneth Kruckemeyer, who had moved to the South End not long before the housing demonstrations started. He became one of the leading activists in the neighborhood in the 1970s and later a deputy to Pangaro in running the entire Southwest Corridor project. "It was part of an awakening of people who were new to the neighborhood to urban issues and urban problems and a coming together of the people who'd lived here for many years."

For more than a decade, protests intended to get the city to follow through on its commitment to build new housing in the South End continued. Meanwhile, the neighborhood organized against extending I-95 through the South End. In 1974, Boston made its first stab at trying to develop the Tent City property. Early plans had called for a parking garage and apartment tower on the site. The Boston Redevelopment Authority decided to require that only 10 percent of the apartments that would be built be affordable to low-income people. "Folks went through the roof," Kruckemeyer remembers. "There was nothing to guarantee that the bulk of the housing built would serve the people that were displaced to create it and nothing to ensure that it would be physically appropriate for this historic neighborhood."

The people of the South End responded with a task force, co-chaired by Kruckemeyer and Mel King, who later became one of Boston's most prominent black leaders. The task force drafted a set of "development principles" that ended up shaping development in the South End a decade later. There were fifteen items in the development principles. They boiled down to two simple bottom lines: Any housing built on the Tent City parcel would have to be affordable to a "full mix" of neighborhood residents; and the physical design of the project would have to "relate closely" to the existing row houses and streetscape.

The redevelopment agency received three proposals to build on the Tent City site. None were acceptable under the South End's development guidelines. The neighborhood took issue again. By that time, residents had enough clout to block any development to which they objected strongly. In any event, the test of wills never came.

Massachusetts's dire financial situation in the mid-1970s put all of the development schemes on ice.

All was quiet until the late 1970s. Thirteen dilapidated buildings stood on the otherwise empty Tent City parcel. A few were owned privately; the rest were in the hands of the city. A large parking lot weaved around buildings on the property. The lot was owned by William Fitzgerald, the retired city fire commissioner, for his Fitz-Inn Autopark.

At one point, Tunny Lee, an MIT urban planning professor who had taken an active interest in the corridor project and was a key player in schooling many of the participants in the art of community participation, decided to use the Tent City site as a studio for his students. They developed alternative development models for the parcel. (One of the students ended up becoming the executive director of the Tent City group in the early 1980s.)

In the late 1970s, Urban Investment and Development Corporation, the developer of Chicago's swank Water Tower Place retail project and one of the nation's leading builders of upscale downtown projects, began pushing plans to build a huge new retail–entertainment–hotel development across from the Tent City property. The project opened as Copley Place in 1984, largely on decking created over the adjacent Massachusetts Turnpike. The state government, which controlled the air rights over the freeway, insisted that Urban Investment and Development "win" its right to a long-term lease by negotiating an agreement with the surrounding neighborhoods. From 1977 to 1980, in fifty public hearings with Back Bay and South End interests, Urban's man-on-site, Gary Himmel, labored over terms. Some sessions, especially in early stages, boiled over into shouting and impassioned controversy.

Four hundred people poured into one meeting at the Boston Public Library, and there were sharp questions: Would Copley Place's sheer mass overpower the nearby streets and row houses? What would be the impact on local traffic, parking, and pedestrian access? Would the buildings cast shadows and stir up winds? What would Urban do for low- and moderate-income housing needs? Who would get the jobs—in construction and then the six thousand-some permanent positions?

Himmel later acknowledged he had been shaken by the intensity of neighborhood demands, but as his "adversaries" became his design advisers, his attitude shifted. His architects actually worked with citizen guidelines tacked up at their work desks. Urban Investment and Development eventually agreed to modify its design to move the taller buildings back from the street, even though the project still overpowers the surrounding low-rise neighborhood.

Twenty percent of the construction jobs were reserved for minorities. Of the project's six thousand permanent jobs, 50.0 percent were earmarked for Boston residents, which included 50.0 percent women, 30.0 percent minorities, and 17.2 percent people from surrounding neighborhoods.

Eventually, Himmel would say that far from ruining the Copley Place development, the neighborhood input led to a superior project, both economically and aesthetically—a suggestion that even on the periphery of the Southwest Corridor, its new planning ethic was influencing Boston's way of doing things.

The entire neighborhood transition raised, predictably enough, broad concerns in the South End. Kruckemeyer explains:

> The heart of the matter was trying to do things which strengthened the neighborhood in transportation and housing and made it better. It pained me to see that good transportation and nice physical design displaced the people you were supposed to be building for. And it was to me irresponsible to say that the poor would have to be condemned to poor transportation and housing because we couldn't figure out a solution. We had to find ways of solving the problem of affordable housing while we were rehabbing the streets in the South End. Here was a way to do quality design, provide service to the neighborhood, and do it all in a way that would stabilize the neighborhood. And we did create a stabilizing influence despite the real estate pressure to gentrify privately owned units. Affordable housing can be done in a way that's stable and good, both socially and physically.

Exactly what would be built on the Tent City parcel became part of both the Southwest Corridor rebuilding effort and the Copley Place development negotiations. There followed several more years of negotiations—with the owner of the parking lot, the city, the developers of Copley Place, and others. Finally, a year and a half after rejecting a complicated deal with the Tent City group to sell the parking lot for $1.25 million and develop housing and parking on the site, the Fitzgerald interests sold the property to Urban Investment and Development. The price tag: $3 million.

Kruckemeyer picks up the narrative, sitting at a battered table in a meeting room in the Tent City apartment building:

> What was Urban Investment and Development going to do with the property? They wanted more parking for Copley Place, about 1,100 spaces on the site. The neighborhood went bananas again. We'd been at it for 14 years. We tried negotiating but pulled out, thinking that having more than 1,000 parking spaces on the property just wouldn't work. That left us with some unhappy people in the city and unhappy developers who'd been seeing dollar signs in their eyes and parking in their future. The neighborhood held enough cards to stop it and hold out for something that it wanted.

The question of affordable housing in the South End had become a pressing issue. During the 1970s and 1980s, as the value of residential real estate in many parts of Boston skyrocketed, the attractive row houses of the South End began drawing young middle- and upper-middle-class families. Displacement, brought on by gentrification and the accompanying conversion of apartments into condominiums, threatened many longtime residents.

Finally, in the mid-1980s, with work on the Southwest Corridor starting to wind down and a beautiful park taking shape next to the Tent City property, the city, neighborhood, and developers negotiated a deal to develop the property. Urban Investment and Development was allowed to build about seven hundred underground parking spaces on the site, 130 of which were reserved for Tent City and the remainder of which could be used for Copley Place parking. The developers would build the underground garage. Tent City would use a variety of public funds to build low- and moderate-income housing. Ground for the new building was broken in 1985.

So the Tent City site came to be occupied by 269 handsome apartments housed in a large, low-rise, red-brick structure that blended in impeccably with the surrounding neighborhood. One-fourth of the residents were poor; half had moderate incomes. The remaining one-fourth of the apartments were rented at "market rate"—which in the fashionable South End of the 1990s translated into $800 monthly for a one-bedroom apartment, running up to $1,700 for a four-bedroom unit. The rich and poor, elderly and young mixed together throughout the new apartment complex. Virtually the only rule distributing apartments by location was the one that gave families with children first crack at ground-floor apartments so that children could play outside with family supervision. People began moving into the new building in April 1988, almost twenty years to the day of the first demonstration on the site.

Back in Tony Pangaro's office along the Charles, the snow was letting up and subway trains running from downtown Boston to Cambridge continued to clatter periodically across the dowdy old Longfellow Bridge.

"It really is possible to find out what people have on their minds and develop an inclusive process," Pangaro said. He glanced out the window at another passing subway train and the Boston skyline, which had come back into view as the snow abated:

> If you can agree on the goals you can work out how they are accomplished. . . . But no matter how good you are about listening to people, you have to remember than you can't substitute a new government for the existing one. You find a way to augment the process. This would never have worked if we'd set up a superauthority to control the whole process.

If we had tried to go and get money and power and invent a new form of government, we'd never had gotten the thing done. Our job was to persuade people, politically and technically, and help them get the money. We wouldn't overrun them. We didn't make a single state legislator or city councilman mad. We didn't have to fight those battles. That empowers people in the neighborhoods. It gives them access to government and helps them be more effective without redoing government.

## *Commentary: Boston*

POLLY WELCH: What is remarkable about this success story is the amount of risk-taking, the political balancing among competing needs, the collaborative process. An example: How do you balance a systemwide problem like transit against the need for local input? It would have been easy for a band of engineers to design the transit system in the abstract from the top down. Any time you allow local input, you create that tension between being able to build something cheap and uniform and building something that responds to the individualized needs of local communities.

JOSEPH P. RILEY, JR.: That's what stunned me: the enormous individuality of design. They didn't try to say, "We have one good idea and we'll run it all the way down the line." Every green space, retail outlet, train station, and sidewalk showed the creation of a public realm with individual character. It was more expensive but it was better. The success is in people finding out they can create a public realm themselves, in this case, a marvelous, complex linear park with both transit and flower gardens.

WELCH: Another important example of balance is the decision to spend less money on the stations and more on parkland. The engineers and architects may have preferred to build a "signature" building for each station. They were not permitted to. There were strict guidelines as to materials, color systems, and technical details. Money was spent to customize station design when it would benefit the life of the community. That was the trade-off and it was based on what designers heard at the participatory meetings. It's important to credit citizen participation as central to the success of this project.

RILEY: Any good architect, planner, or lawyer will tell you that they do their best work when their client is well-prepared. Give me a client that understands the facts of the situation and I can do a better job in the courtroom. Give a designer a community that has thought through the details and he or she will be able to create alternatives.

STEVE LIVINGSTON: The diversity was so great that this can't be called a project. It was many projects linked together over thirty years with government and citizen participation. One of the challenges in urban redevelopment is sustaining government support for thirty years and more.

RILEY: In this generation, the popular model is the suburban model. You have a cornfield and then, almost overnight, you have a regional shopping mall, a cloverleaf, and a mixed-use complex; but in building and rebuilding cities, you must have patience, put it into a historical context, and then do the hard political work.

WELCH: The theme of this project is "healing the scar." The scar is physical, social, economic. Each of these dimensions was addressed—which is what the Rudy Bruner Award is about. The scale of the project is mind-boggling. It had an impact on one-third of the city's population.

Boston had already been through two major urban renewal projects: one in the Back Bay for the Convention Center and one downtown for the Government Center in the old West End, the subject of Herb Gans's *The Urban Villagers*. The city already had sacrificed a community to show its willingness to embrace urban renewal. The idea of tearing down more neighborhoods for "progress" was not a new issue. People were familiar with the social and personal cost.

The other piece of the scar was the railroad: a divider between the haves and have-nots. It linked Boston to the rest of the world but divided its neighborhoods. Transit systems aren't built just to bring people into and out of a city. The new rail system represents a conscious effort to link the people on opposite sides of the tracks. The participatory process was one where people had to confront their prejudices along with their need to get across to the other side.

RILEY: A city is an ecosystem. You have to respect its power and its delicacy. You must respect, for example, that in decking over a transit rail line to create a public space, a planner's egalitarian notion of interaction may disturb the city's balance. The Boston plan was successful because so many citizens were involved, particularly in deciding these details of where—and where not—to deck.

WELCH: The issue of getting across the system also involved this question: If people used it as a recreation path, where would they exit the system and whose street would they end up on? As it turned out, the first third is completely decked over. You get a linear park, and one is unaware of what's below. In the second third, in Roxbury, where there's quite a bit of decking, that community chose carefully where it thought the deck would be useful in creating recreation areas and where they could forego it. The third part has much less decking, and what there is is primarily near the subway stations.

LIVINGSTON: Managers and designers of public spaces realize that something magic happens to people in a space that is working. People are transformed. The magic was allowed to happen in Boston by matching the design to both young and old, to various ethnic groups.

WELCH: One of the social problems inherent in mass transit is that people in more affluent communities at the end of the rail line are afraid of inner-city people using the line to come into their neighborhoods. It was the middle of the line in Boston that had the poorest people, in the Roxbury section. People at both ends of the line were worried that this would have an impact on their neighborhoods.

An additional problem was to balance regional versus local transit needs. Part of the purpose of the line was to get suburbanites into the city without their cars, to make it attractive and convenient to them.

There's also the issue of parkland management. The city has built itself a wonderful green space, but there's an ongoing discussion about how it's going to be maintained and by whom.

LIVINGSTON: The management begins in the design process. Design addresses physical needs but it also addresses participation. People adopt the space at that initial point in the process. Security and maintenance are easier if that foundation of participation is there. Public spaces conjure up fears, but you can handle that through participation in the planning process.

WELCH: The Southwest Corridor project is not yet complete. There are loose ends, as with any large-scale undertaking. Sometimes it is difficult to resolve problems and ensure financial and political support once the project is publically declared complete. Completion and sustainability ideally go hand in hand.

The Metropolitan District Commission, which was going to manage the parklands, experienced drastic budget cuts. In addition, several community task forces wanted the parkland managed at the local rather than the regional level so that they could continue to have the input that they'd had in the planning process. They felt if vandalism were a problem, it could be solved more effectively at a local level. They felt that community gardens shouldn't be managed by a regionwide agency that is too far removed from the users to work out problems.

This project raises the question of how people continue to feel a sense of ownership and pride over these hundreds of acres of green space over time. Part of the answer in this era of "a thousand points of light" is volunteerism. As with Cabrillo Village, those who don't remember the hours it took to create something may have less understanding of, and appreciation for, its benefit to their lives.

Southwest Corridor also raises the issue of how you sustain political support to make sure the promises get fulfilled. The city of Boston has a concept called linkage. It requires that developers who want to construct new buildings downtown have to contribute linkage money for development of buildings in economically depressed neighborhoods.

A large parcel adjacent to the corridor in Roxbury remains vacant and undeveloped because the city and the state struggle in their collaborative effort to get it completed. In a public housing development abutting the corridor, the housing authority and tenant task force have chosen to leave the housing units closest to the subway boarded up as a clear message that they have not yet received the state and local funds to complete the housing renewal work.

**RILEY:** Money alone is not going to do it, and grass-roots involvement won't do it if you don't have the money.

Cities represent a civilization's statement about their times. You enrich a civilization, and often its poorest people, when you make it possible for quality investments to be made in the city. You lift the tide in the city with programs like the Urban Development Action Grant, and you lift all boats, rural and urban. That's why it is so regrettable when such programs are abandoned.

**WELCH:** Yet another imaginative dimension of the Southwest Corridor development was the education and training component that got inner-city kids working in the offices of the project design consultants and engineers so they could learn skills and experience professions they might not otherwise know about.

MIT and Harvard faculty and students played a role. The Southwest Corridor project was a perfect field setting for design students to be exposed to the realities of participatory design. In fact, one of the positive outcomes of the project is that now there is, in effect, a class of "Southwest Corridor" graduates in architecture, planning, and urban design who got their feet wet, got their first real world experience, and developed their professional values by devoting a piece of their lives to this project. They are now the current generation of movers and shakers.

CHAPTER 4

# *Lincoln's Radial Reuse: A Quiet Plains Revolution*

February in Lincoln, a time of year when the checkerboard of cornfields on the outskirts of Nebraska's capital city is still a somber brown and everyone is patiently waiting out the last two months of the Great Plains winter. On this particular Thursday afternoon, the mercury is pushing a non-Nebraska sixty degrees and the skies are a deep, crystal-clear prairie blue. Only the faint contrails of a high-flying plane cut the stunning azure sky.

Spring has come to Lincoln, at least temporarily. And in Clinton, a residential enclave of unpretentious, salt-of-the-earth homes north of downtown and the towering limestone shaft of the state capitol building, the premature warmth has transformed the neighborhood into a beehive of activity.

On Twenty-first Street, a quiet working-class block, carpenters are putting the finishing touches on a light-gray, two-story home. The house used to sit across town, a dilapidated eyesore marked for bulldozing, until the city arranged to have the building moved to this new site. Several blocks away, workers are carrying two-by-fours around the side of a gleaming one-story, white, wood-frame house. Before the renovation work hit the home stretch, the little house was an unkempt mess of rotting wood and peeling paint.

On Potter Street, workers are carrying building materials in and out of another home that used to be unfit for habitation. Children's toys, in pink and purple, are scattered around the brown front lawn. A newly completed bike path and park, the linchpin of Lincoln's redevelopment scheme for Clinton and two other bedraggled neighborhoods, push up against the home's backyard. On yet another corner, a gang of young boys and girls is having a time of it. They are laughing and playing and moving dirt from a gaping hole scheduled to become the foundation of a new home.

Woodside Park, on Clinton's northern boundary, is also new. A handful of neighborhood children are enjoying themselves on the park's playground equipment, but otherwise the neighborhood is quiet. In the soft pink light of this midwinter late afternoon, the park frames a tableau of towering grain elevators, a staple of the landscape throughout the Plains.

Heartland industry and the railroads that sent their products out across America built Clinton into a bedrock working-class community in the 1800s. To the south, Clinton is still hemmed in by many of those same industries, but today they are struggling to keep Nebraska's sputtering agribusiness machine running. A little north and west, a wide corridor of rail lines heads out of town in every direction. Farther west looms the University of Nebraska and its vast campus, dominated by the football stadium that becomes the Cornhusker State's third-largest city on game days.

Ten years ago, Clinton was not a solid working-class neighborhood, it was a neighborhood teetering on an abyss. Its population fell 20 percent from 1960 to 1980, even though Lincoln as a whole was growing. About 60 percent of Clinton's residents were renters in 1980; back in 1960, 60 percent were homeowners. Many of Clinton's streets were dirt paths. They turned into muddy streams after rainfalls.

Clinton, circa 1980, had the texture of abandonment—not the kind of apocalyptic urban ruin of the South Bronx or Chicago's South Side but a more genteel Lincoln version of city rot. The neighborhood was marred by block upon block of run-down homes, empty lots overrun with weeds, and scattered, occupied old homes, many of them in advanced stages of disrepair.

However, Clinton recovered in time for the 1990s. Slowly and painstakingly, it regained the feel of a stable, working-class, middle-American community—and not by accident. The invisible hand and guiding intelligence behind the resurrection of Clinton was a city government program known officially as the Radial Reuse Project. The plan included a four-mile-long, eight-foot-wide concrete bike and walking path surrounded by soft prairie landscaping. Five neighborhood ("nodal") parks, such as Woodside Park, were placed at key junctures along the path. The bike path, parks, and playgrounds were at the center of something much grander, though. The Radial Reuse Project, hashed out over nearly ten years of community planning and participation, became, in reality, a comprehensive revitalization scheme for Lincoln's most run-down neighborhoods.

In addition to Clinton, one of Lincoln's most venerable neigh-

***The critical link in the Radial Reuse Project: a four-mile bike and walking path that connects five neighborhood parks.*** *(Photograph courtesy of Roger Bruhn, Lincoln, Nebraska)*

borhoods, the park and trail cut through two other old neighborhoods. One of those was University Place, a more affluent and dignified neighborhood to Clinton's east that adjoins the eastern campus of the University of Nebraska. Originally an independent town, University Place was annexed by Lincoln in the 1920s. Its old city hall, on the neighborhood's main shopping street, still stands strangely as a monument to those bygone days.

Due south of Clinton is Malone, a tattered old black and working-class neighborhood hard against the university's main campus. Parts of Malone have been periodically gobbled up by the university's fits and starts of expansion. Students look to Malone for cheap housing. Slumlords have used it to build ugly little real estate empires. Change was to come to Malone, too, but at the start of the 1990s, it still displayed all of the scars of decades of decline, uncertainty, and abandonment.

With about 200,000 people, Lincoln is a lucky town. As Nebraska's preeminent university town and state capital, it has been spared the wrenching boom-and-bust cycles experienced by so many cities. It has benefited, ironically, from the decline of smaller Nebraska towns, whose residents have been obliged to flee the land and farming in favor of such "big" cities as Lincoln.

Southern Lincoln is prosperous. Big suburban-style homes and ramblers fronted by perfectly manicured lawns flank tree-lined streets. Northern Lincoln—known locally as the part of town "north of O Street" or, less kindly, as "the wrong side of the tracks"—has suffered a different fate.

Radial Reuse is a story of nearly forty years of planning, politics, struggles, defeats, and victories. It began with a plan to build a highway out of downtown Lincoln through Clinton, Malone, University Place, and the northeastern suburbs with the hope that they would prosper like the neighborhoods in the southern part of town. Radial Reuse became a lesson in how those civic plans for development in the 1950s went awry and ended up leading to deterioration and decline in the 1960s and 1970s. It would become a plot with such unlikely heros as the angry housewives who started organizing in the 1960s and ended up kindling a fire that revolutionized local politics and changed Lincoln's power structure forever. By the late 1980s, it was culminating in the carefully planned revival of the three neighborhoods that the original highway plan would have sliced into pieces.

Radial Reuse ultimately is the story of how ordinary citizens organized, later generations of political leaders battled, and city bureaucrats unceasingly worked to undo damage caused by three decades of scheming, neglect, and indecision at city hall.

## *Long Road to Ruin*

When the long saga of Clinton, Malone, and University Place began, Harry S. Truman was finishing out his last year in the Oval Office. Dwight D. Eisenhower and Richard M. Nixon were on the campaign trail against Adlai Stevenson. The United States was embroiled in a war in Korea. The Berlin Wall, the Kennedy assassination, and Vietnam were still a decade away. Ronald Reagan was really just a movie actor.

The year was 1952. Envisioning potential growth on the city's north side, Lincoln's city fathers settled on what then seemed like the perfect tonic: a four-lane, divided highway to provide a fast link to the neighborhoods and developing suburbs to the north and east of downtown. This was, after all, the beginning of the era of America's love affair with the automobile and the dawn of the highway building boom that was to continue clear through the 1970s.

Slowly, Lincoln began buying up property in Clinton, Malone, and University Place for what was to be the Northeast Radial Highway, a counterpart to a roadway running from downtown to the southeast part of town. An acre here. An acre there. A zigzag patchwork of land in a rough line where the Northeast Radial Highway was supposed to go. By the time the city stopped acquiring property for the road in the early 1970s, it owned about seventy-five acres of land in the three neighborhoods. The homes on the city-owned land were either demolished or left to sit vacant and decaying while the highway building plans wended their way toward approval.

As plans to build the highway proceeded, the University of Nebraska, always a political giant in Lincoln, began preparing a dramatic campus expansion. Many residents expected that the university's Board of Regents wanted to link, at some point in the future, their main campus with their east campus located several miles away in University Place. The Radial Highway seemed like a perfect way to speed up the expansion and future campus merger.

What occurred, however, was quite different. The highway plans began to stall and sputter in the early 1960s, not long after they were first announced. Not everyone in Lincoln was sold on the idea that the Northeast Radial Highway was needed. The ultimate result was neither what the city nor the university had intended. Former Lincoln City Councilman Eric Youngberg, a man who came to town as a VISTA (Volunteers in Service to America) volunteer and ended up leading the movement to organize the three neighborhoods to stop the Radial Highway, summarized the impact quite tersely: "The city and the university, in effect, created a slum."

What started out as a prideful municipal exercise to foster growth started showing its first civic cracks quickly. Between the time Lincoln's comprehensive plan was adopted in 1951 and a city transportation study was done in 1967, plans to build the roadway proceeded, if slowly and incrementally, but tinkering with the highway plan was already under way. Slowly, painfully, and piece by piece, stretches of the proposed highway were put on the chopping block, and when Lincoln's comprehensive plan was revised in 1977, large hunks of roadway were well on their way to being amputated. Road or no road, however, the city clung to the property it had acquired along the full length of the hoped-for highway.

Even with the fast clip of redevelopment in the early 1990s, there was still a stark, visible difference between the property within the route of the Radial Highway and the areas outside of its path. The old proposed highway corridor was like a slowly healing scar:

empty land, decayed homes, and unkempt blocks that the Radial Reuse Project was painstakingly cleaning up. Land immediately outside the corridor showed, by contrast, a semblance of normalcy: neater homes, lawns mowed, clearer evidence that property owners and residents exercised care.

The reasons for the disparities were simple. Land earmarked for the Radial Highway had been deliberately excluded from city housing rehabilitation programs and infrastructure improvements. Clinton, Malone, and University Place became neighborhoods non grata. They were cut off from such critical federal money as hundreds of thousands of dollars available locally through the Community Development Block Grant program. Even worse, many neighborhood leaders said, were the debilitating effects of twenty years of indecision and uncertainty about whether or not the roadway would ever be built. Clinton, Malone, and University Place were never Lincoln's choicest addresses. With the ever-present threat of the highway, the neighborhoods gained an even greater stigma.

Slowly but surely, the consequences started showing. Property owners did not invest in homes that might be demolished. Repairs were not made. On city-owned property, buildings rotted and weeds grew. People voted with their feet and started moving out.

Clinton, Malone, and University Place were overshadowed by that dark cloud hovering ominously in the sky, the Northeast Radial Highway. Dolores Lintel, one of the original neighborhood organizers against the highway proposal, minced no words in making the point and directing the finger of blame. Despite her normally quiet housewife's voice, her restrained anger was unmistakable as she described the fate of Clinton, the neighborhood where she bought a home in 1960: "The streets were in lousy shape and buses were being routed around us," Lintel said. "No repairs were being made on the houses the city bought and it was becoming a blighted and neglected part of town. We were angry. We felt betrayed and we felt used."

In the late 1960s and early 1970s, Lintel continued, "We called it benign neglect. The trees weren't being trimmed. The building codes weren't being enforced. The city had just written us off. Who wants to move into a neighborhood that's going to be destroyed, where the houses are bad and the schools aren't being upgraded?"

Diane Morgan, one of the city officials responsible for coordinating the redevelopment project, flatly admitted that by 1980: "The city was aggravating the situation with every year that passed. There were a lot of justifiably bitter feelings toward the city government."

As time went on, residents such as Lintel and Youngberg and their neighbors became angrier and angrier. In response to citizen pressure, the city shortened the Radial Highway even more in 1979, removing much of the roadway that would have sliced cavalierly through the heart of Clinton. Clinton's budding neighborhood organization presented residents with a number of options, ranging from building the highway to allowing a smaller roadway to building nothing at all. They voted to nix the roads. Lincoln complied, but only partly. It removed the Clinton segment of the highway from the city plan. On another level, the power politics of the thing called the Northeast Radial Highway continued unabated.

Yet by the early 1980s, nearly three decades after the idea first surfaced, not a spade of dirt had been turned, not an inch of pavement laid. By then, the projected cost of the shortened road had skyrocketed to $18 million. The odds were growing dimmer with each passing day that a new highway of *any* length would ever be built. Former Lincoln Mayor Helen G. Boosalis, who presided over city hall from 1975 to 1983, concluded that the Radial Highway was "too expensive, too grandiose, unnecessary, and damaging to the neighborhoods through which the corridor had been routed."

Had the roadway been built when it was proposed, suggested Coleen J. Seng, a University Place neighborhood activist and Lincoln City Council member starting in 1987, "it would have been welcomed. In fact, it probably should have been built. But it wasn't, and by the time everybody got around to deciding to build it no one wanted it any more."

The city's 1979 move to lop off the Clinton part of the highway—at least on paper—did prove to be the beginning of the end for the Radial Highway. It was also the opening salvo in an equally long and contentious struggle to figure out how to undo damage already done.

The same year the Clinton stretch of highway vanished from the city planner's maps, the city appointed its Radial Reuse Task Force, setting in motion a planning process that would ultimately span three different mayors and five different city councils. The group was a citizens' advisory body charged with coming up with alternatives for the ribbonlike highway right-of-way the city had amassed since 1952. The city council went out of its way to direct that the group allow for maximum citizen participation in its deliberations. Notably, the task force was not ordered to debate whether the road should or should not be built. By that point, it was a foregone conclusion that the Northeast Radial Highway was nearing its death throes.

Twelve citizen members of the task force were appointed by

Mayor Boosalis and the city council to represent a spectrum of community interests. The task force included, among others, four "citizens-at-large," three representatives from the neighborhoods the highway would have cut through, and two representatives from the business community. In 1981, another five members joined the group, including emissaries from the University of Nebraska and the Chamber of Commerce.

Gordon Scholz, the soft-spoken chairman of the department of community and regional planning at the University of Nebraska, was the Radial Reuse Task Force's first chairman in the rough and tumble days of the late 1970s. He explained the group's initial choice this way:

> The question was whether the [highway] right-of-way was going to be a liability or an asset. As vacant land it wasn't doing anything to stimulate confidence or investment in the neighborhoods. One option was for the city simply to sell all the land to the highest bidder and be done with it. Other people were saying "Let's turn this into an amenity and an asset." Fortunately that idea prevailed. The simplest thing to do would have been to sell the land and not struggle through the process of deciding what we were going to do. One can only speculate what would have happened if the land had just been sold off to the highest bidder.

One of the first things the task force did was invite a Regional/Urban Design Assistance Team (R/UDAT) from the American Institute of Architects to study the neighborhoods and the options. The R/UDAT prowled Lincoln and held meetings for four days. It concluded the highway plan should be scrapped in its entirety and that the city take immediate action to stabilize the neighborhoods. "You either sacrifice the neighborhood . . . or you choose to save it," said one of the R/UDAT members at the end of the session. "Our recommendation is to save it."

In 1980, after months of rancorous debate, the city council voted to deep-six the Northeast Radial Highway. Within twenty-four hours, Willard Woodside, president of the Lincoln Citizens Association (and, incidentally, the gentleman for whom Woodside Park was later named despite his prohighway sentiments), announced a petition drive to put the Radial Highway to a ballot vote.

The University of Nebraska, builders, developers, and assorted downtown business interests got behind the ballot initiative to borrow money to build the highway. Voters were asked to build the highway out to the length suggested by the 1965 transit study—the route that cut through Clinton, which the city had already removed from its plans. Neighborhood groups across the city fought back—and hard. Even though the proponents of the highway outspent them by eight to one, voters opted to send the Northeast Radial Highway down the road to oblivion by a three-to-two margin. In December 1981, on the heels of the "no build" public vote, the city council voted to remove the entire Northeast Radial Highway from Lincoln's comprehensive plan and from the budget as well. Nearly thirty years after the idea was first hatched, the highway was finally and definitively dead and gone.

With the highway monster finally vanquished, there began an equally tough chapter: figuring out what to do with seventy-five acres of city-owned ex-right-of-way, and how to treat three rapidly deteriorating neighborhoods. The task was firmly in the hands of the Radial Reuse Task Force. Ultimately, it came up with a deceptively simple solution—the city should mix residential and industrial redevelopment and use a linear park to separate the two land uses along the radial corridor in Clinton, Malone, and University Place. The city council ratified the plans in their entirety in 1984.

The plan, as enacted, had seven major goals:

- To stimulate private residential and business reinvestment.
- To provide needed recreation and open space.

***A deceptively simple idea: a linear park to act as a buffer between residential and industrial uses.*** *(Photograph courtesy of Roger Bruhn, Lincoln, Nebraska)*

- To make the infrastructure improvements desperately needed in the neighborhoods.
- To open up new opportunities for existing businesses to expand and to lure new businesses.
- To provide home ownership opportunities for low- and moderate-income Lincoln families.
- To resolve the simmering and bitter land-use conflicts between the University of Nebraska and the adjacent Malone neighborhood.
- To try to rebuild a positive image for all three neighborhoods.

"The thrust of the plan was to use the city's land to revitalize the neighborhoods and to instill confidence back in people that the city was serious about rebuilding," said Dallas McGee, the Lincoln community development official who oversaw the redevelopment plan. The plan committed the city to building the bicycle path and parks on the land once earmarked for the highway. It also obliged the city to spend even more money buying up land that the city had missed in its first passes through the neighborhoods. Massive infrastructure improvements, including long-awaited street paving, were scheduled. The city set aside money for housing rehabilitation and committed itself to building housing on vacant lots and making redevelopment parcels available to developers. All these efforts were intended to lure private investment back into the three neighborhoods.

"Our assumption when we were developing the plan for the amenities in the corridor was that their presence would stimulate positive economic investment in the adjacent areas," former task force chief Scholz explained. "People would begin to see these neighborhoods as desirable places to live, invest, or have a business. A positive environment pays off economically."

The city decided to start in University Place, reasoning it was the least deteriorated of the three neighborhoods in the path of the highway. By the start of the 1990s, work in that neighborhood was complete, and renovation work in Clinton was nearly finished, too. The bicycle path and parks were also complete in both neighborhoods. Work was starting in Malone, the most run-down of all of the neighborhoods. The entire project was scheduled for completion in 1992, exactly forty years after the Northeast Radial Highway became part of the vocabulary in Lincoln.

## *The Housewives Who Started the Fire*

Sitting back in a chair in a city office building, Dolores Lintel, gray-haired and modestly dressed, does not look the part of a revolutionary. She fits the part of a loving midwestern grandmother, which she is, not Che Guevara, but Lintel, who moved to the city with her husband in 1956, turned out to be Lincoln's grandmotherly version of Che.

The first shots in the revolution of Lincoln politics were fired at Saturday morning coffee klatches organized by Lintel. It was 1964, and she and other housewives in Clinton started meeting every week to sip coffee, talk, and figure out what was happening in their neighborhood:

> We didn't have any idea of what was happening or why, although residents were aware that the city government was buying real estate in their neighborhood. But we decided that we would have to take responsibility for our neighborhood and not leave it up to the city.

***Lintel Park. At neighborhood coffee klatches that she organized, Dolores Lintel fired the first shots in the revolution of Lincoln's politics.*** *(Photograph courtesy of Roger Bruhn, Lincoln, Nebraska)*

It did not take long before the informal Saturday morning coffee sessions turned into scheduled weekly neighborhood meetings in the basement of the local school. The group followed a "start small" theory of community organizing. The first goal—a modest exercise in political muscle flexing—was convincing the city to fix up an alley next to their local school. The alley was a bumpy strip full of gaping potholes. Lintel and her allies raised a ruckus. The city filled the potholes. The alley was fixed up. The battle of the potholes won, the fledgling neighborhood activists started getting involved in zoning cases. They began fighting requests to build high-density apartment buildings in their predominantly single-family-home neighborhood.

None of this, of course, was planned in advance. As Lintel recalls:

> At each meeting we'd kind of figure out what was the most pressing issue and figure out what to do about it. We just chugged along trying to manage to do something about what was happening to us. We just did what we had to do.

Coleen J. Seng lives in University Place, just a short distance away from Lintel. Seng is a mild-mannered community worker with the First United Methodist Church in Lincoln. Appearances are deceptive. Underneath, she is tough as nails. Seng got her baptism in community organizing under the aegis of the late and legendary Saul Alinsky, the Chicago-based neighborhood organizer whose confrontational tactics forever immortalized him in the community action hall of fame.

Seng speaks the language of an Alinsky descendant:

> Empowerment of people is the foremost issue for neighborhoods. We spent lots and lots of time developing leadership. We had a community full of well-educated people. And we spent a lot of time getting ourselves trained about what to do in the community. That's still the key issue for neighborhood organizations.

Seng entered the fray in the 1970s when she started working with the University Place Community Organization. From 1974 to 1976, she headed the group as it fought to stop street widenings, to get streets paved, to develop parks, to pass sewer bond issues, to organize community festivals in the hope of pulling the community together, and to run garden markets in the summer.

It was not a big leap from those modest beginnings into full-fledged community activism. It was, in Seng's words, as simple as being "sick and tired of having things shoved down our throats."

Lintel, Seng, and their allies first formed a community organization called Impact. Then, in 1976, they organized the Lincoln Alliance, a broad-based coalition of eighteen church and neighborhood groups. "We were coming to the realization that we had power," Lintel would recall years later, still sounding a little bit surprised. By the time the Radial Highway became a white-hot political issue, the Lincoln Alliance had become a force to be reckoned with. Lintel laughs when she recalls the shenanigans she and her cohorts would engage in to get the attention of city politicians. She smiles broadly remembering the times she invited the mayor to come to Clinton on rainy days so that the mayoral automobile would get stuck in the neighborhood's muddy roads.

The political balance of power in Lincoln was starting to change, and it was shifting dramatically. Before 1976, very few neighborhoods had a role in Lincoln's governance. Power was wielded by what neighborhood activists bitterly referred to as "the O Street Gang"—the downtown bankers, developers, and business people who virtually dictated the city's public policy agenda by private fiat. "Those were the tough years," Seng recalls. "It was extremely difficult breaking up the hold the money people had on the city."

Slowly, however, the money people started losing their total sway. As the neighborhoods consolidated around stopping the Radial Highway, political activists—led by VISTA volunteer Youngberg, who was active in Malone—began a drive to revise the makeup of the city council. Traditionally, all seven council members were elected at-large, an arrangement greatly diluting the influence of individual neighborhoods. When the activists were finished stirring up trouble, the council had four "district" representatives and only three at-large members. Youngberg was elected to the city council as the district representative from the Radial Highway neighborhoods. The outsiders suddenly found themselves inside the doors of power.

Helen G. Boosalis, a staunch supporter of citizen involvement and participation, was elected mayor in 1975. Her "basic philosophy was to have open government and citizen involvement in every possible way," former task force chieftain Scholz recalled. "That's what led to this approach of having a task force with as much citizen participation as possible. She wanted to resolve the roadway question. She wasn't in favor of it but she didn't try to squelch debate on it either. That attitude of participation in government was a milestone. She welcomed everyone's participation." (In the 1986 elections, Boosalis was the Democratic party's nominee for governor of Nebraska.)

The participatory spirit and sensitivity that Boosalis and the citizen activists brought to Lincoln city government extended to the implementation of the Radial Reuse redevelopment plan itself. As the city started acquiring the remainder of the land that it needed to complete the linear park and assemble its redevelopment parcels for housing, it purposely refrained from claiming property by eminent domain. Quite the contrary. The city did backflips to meet residents' special requests for holding onto their property "just a little bit longer." One elderly widow, for instance, lived in a home that was in the way of the bicycle path, but there was an odd problem. The widow did not want to budge. Her husband had perished in an accident in a nearby grain elevator and she wanted to live out her remaining years in the house, which had a view of the grain elevator where her husband had died. The city of Lincoln obliged. It waited until she died before claiming her property for the path.

In another case, several brothers who owned a nursery wanted to finish out a few more years in business before they finally retired. Again the city complied. When the brothers decided to hang up their spikes for good, the city incorporated their property into the park system. Today the legacy of that nursery—a miniature botanical garden of flora and fauna—is a permanent part of Lincoln's new linear park.

All this made Seng a happy woman. She expressed immense thrill over the outcome of the long, drawn-out Radial Reuse fight. She said she loved her new job on the city council because it gave her, finally, the chance to influence policy from the inside. She noted the stark contrast to earlier years when "we had such polarization between decision makers and the neighborhood folks that communication just wasn't possible."

Through Radial Reuse, in fact, neighborhood participation and communitywide planning became far stronger parts of the decision-making process in Lincoln. Developers learned the practical wisdom of checking in with neighborhood leaders before going ahead with building projects.

Despite her rise to become a bona fide member of the Lincoln establishment, Seng harbored some doubts as the 1990s began. She was afraid that Lincolnites were letting down their guard in the afterglow of stopping the Radial Highway and redeveloping the damaged neighborhoods. She said there had been a precipitous decline in citizen activism, adding:

> We've got to get the citizen's organizations going again. Lincoln is a terribly middle-class, white, middle-income town. We don't rally around a cause too rapidly here unless it's something right in front of our house. There's not an understanding that people still need to work together.

Lintel, who opted out of the political squabbling after the Radial Highway went down in flames in 1981, seemed content, afterward, just to be a grandmother. She freely admitted to having become "burned out" by the public warfare. Still, a wry smile—the kind of smile that bursts with the pride of having fought the good fight—crosses her face when she remembers the battles and the sweet victories she and her neighbors won:

> This was a very grass-roots effort. We were just people who were ready to stand up and be counted and say "We won't let this happen." If we hadn't gotten involved we'd have been just as guilty as everyone else. But the people stood up and said "No way." The people won.

Lintel leaned back in her chair. She was silent for a moment, absorbed in thought, and then she added:

> Anger is a very good motivator. It's a very powerful thing to take that emotion and do something constructive with it.

Out of Radial Reuse, a park came to Clinton—a modest little swath of land with some trees, a gazebo squatting in the middle, and playground equipment scattered about. Everybody in the neighborhood took to calling it "Grandma's Park," and Lintel bursts with pride when she mentions how her little granddaughter takes special pleasure in taking her friends to play in the park. The park is officially called Lintel Park. To Dolores Lintel's granddaughter, it really is "Grandma's Park."

## *Ways, Means, and Returns*

Radial Reuse did not come easily—or cheaply. A hugh menu of city programs had to be applied to make the redevelopment project hum. With the last trees planted and the final nails hammered into new and renovated homes, Lincoln was expected to have invested $6.4 million of public money in Clinton, Malone, and University Place. By 1990, the city calculated that more than $17 million in private investment had flowed into the neighborhoods as well. "The park was designed to encourage redevelopment and that's exactly what happened," said Lincoln community development official McGee.

As part of the redevelopment process, Lincoln's community development department offered up a host of relocation assistance programs aimed at low- and moderate-income families. Most of the assistance was developed in consultation with the neighborhood groups that had fought the Radial Highway and then pushed for the Radial Reuse Plan in the first place.

First, an elaborate system of financial aid was put in place. It included a home purchase assistance program featuring deferred and no-interest loans and, in some cases, even loan forgiveness.

Vacant lots in the neighborhoods were marketed through the city's infill housing program, which offers eligible homeowners low-priced lots. In 1987, in fact, Lincoln started offering some parcels of land for free to families that could get financing, agree to build a home designed to be compatible with the neighborhood, and would promise to live on the lot for at least five years.

The city set up a citizen design review committee for the redevelopment area and a set of "infill" or so-called "slip-in" design guidelines. Design was a major concern because of some past developer abuse—evidenced in a number of sites in Clinton, Malone, and University Place—by old garden-style apartment complexes, called "slip-ins." Charitably stated, the slip-ins resembled rock-bottom budget army barracks. Their backsides, more often than not windowless, faced the local streets. Lincoln's new guidelines sought to assure that new housing, especially multifamily complexes, would comply with the residential character of the neighborhoods and be sensitive to existing neighborhood architecture.

The city set up yet another program to move homes slated for demolition to other plots of land where they could be renovated much less expensively than building from scratch. By 1990, some seventeen homes had made the ungainly, slow trek from their old sites to their new digs. More were scheduled to be moved, saving low- and moderate-income homes from likely dates with a bulldozer.

To the naked eye, the results of all this effort and expense are obvious, even simple. The park system itself is a modest greenway skirting Clinton and University Place. The bikeway and park serve as a "buffer" between homes and the industrial and railroad traffic to their north. Scattered throughout the trail are framed views of grain elevators, trains, and parks. The concrete path and park nodes are not fancy or flashy by any standard. They simply work. The landscaping is not extraordinary. In fact, it is the kind of work that would probably make a *New York Times* architectural critic blanch. It is all simple, relatively low-maintenance planting and grass with little or no pretense of being anything else. It is all decidedly residential and human in scale and character. It is Lincoln.

By the Lincoln city government's reckoning, development encouraged by the park system and the Reuse Plan resulted in 446 new, relocated, or rehabilitated homes, most of them for families with modest incomes. The city could point to twenty-seven blocks of repaved streets (putting a conclusive end to the muddy street phenomenon). By 1990, fifteen businesses in the redevelopment area had expanded, adding 222 permanent jobs. Another eight new businesses had set up shop with fifty-one new jobs. Money was starting to flow back into the city coffers. From the start of the renovation work to the end of the 1980s, the value of the tax rolls increased more than 28 percent in Clinton and University Place.

## *Malone: The Final Battleground*

Malone, the neighborhood that adjoins the University of Nebraska's main campus and is closest to downtown, is Lincoln's reality check, its perennial problem child, and a stark reminder of what the parts of Clinton and University Place that have already been redeveloped used to look like. In Malone, early 1990, vacant land was still one of the most prominent staples of the landscape. Decrepit homes were abundant. Some sat on land that would soon be turned into a park. In short, it was the perfect picture of old-fashioned deterioration.

One large, vacant area was a redevelopment parcel where new homes were destined to go up, but many of the homes in Malone were boarded up, just the way they have been for years. On some blocks, plywood was the predominant window covering. On one street sat a little white house looking like a real estate agent's worst nightmare. A huge "No Trespassing" sign covered the door. Mattresses and trash were strewn about what used to be a front lawn.

Malone grew up in the late 1800s as a single-family residential neighborhood for doctors, university professors, businessmen, and other middle-income workers. By the turn of the century it "was socially heterogeneous, with university professors, railroad mechanics, company vice presidents and janitors living near each other," according to the *Historic and Architectural Site Survey of Malone* (Lincoln, NE: University of Nebraska, College of Architecture, 1980). "Gradually, however, the presence of white-collar workers in the neighborhood diminished due in part to the rising prestige of the residential areas opening in the southeast part of the city after World War II."

So began a long decline that could not be blamed entirely on the Northeast Radial Highway or the University of Nebraska. Malone had long represented the poorest neighborhood in Lincoln. The median income of Malone residents sank to $7,000, compared with a citywide median of $14,700. About 17 percent of Malone's residents were black. The neighborhood's population dropped from 3,908 to 2,724. The owner occupancy rate, meanwhile, plummeted from 40 percent to a mere 19 percent.

In the mid-1970s, a local housing survey took a look at Malone and reached a disturbing conclusion: fully 83 percent of the housing in Malone, the researchers determined, was "deteriorated." While Malone did not become a racial enclave in the strictest sense of the word, the black-white division remained vivid. Blacks and poor people were clustered in the neighborhood's particularly shabby southwestern corner. Younger, more affluent whites lived in the eastern half of the neighborhood, farthest from the downtown university campus. Many of the residents were students living in single-family homes that had been converted into apartments or in apartment buildings that replaced single-family homes.

Of all of Lincoln's troubled neighborhoods, Malone had to fight more battles simultaneously than any other. It was perennially threatened by the University of Nebraska's ambitions of physical expansion. In some ways, the plan to run the highway through the neighborhood was just one more nail in the coffin. Years later, many neighborhood residents still chafed when they remembered how

***Visible progress. In the mid-1970s, a survey concluded that 83 percent of housing in the Malone neighborhood was deteriorated.*** *(Photograph courtesy of Roger Bruhn, Lincoln, Nebraska)*

they had once expected the university to kick all of its fraternities off campus and exile them to Malone.

To fight off the double-barreled threat of the university's voracious appetite for land and the Northeast Radial Highway, residents organized the Malone Area Citizens Council in 1976; it became the Malone Neighborhood Association in 1985. "There were so many negative influences on Malone: the university and its expansion plans, the Radial Highway plan, a crime rate that kept rising, and the devaluation of property," noted Gregory D. Newport, an architect who brought a house in Malone in 1982 and went on to become one of the leaders of the neighborhood association. Malone, Newport said, "sank into a pit of despair." He described his experience in the neighborhood as "seven years of renovating a house and a neighborhood along with personal renovation."

Malone was included in the final 1984 Radial Reuse Plan. The details of land use in the neighborhood had been worked out between the city, residents, and the university, but things changed. In 1986, the university started to rethink its expansion plans again. It wanted a bigger hunk of Malone than the Radial Reuse Plan allowed for and it declared the 1984 plan dead.

So began the final and perhaps bloodiest battle of the entire redevelopment process in Lincoln. "It was more than clear that the university wanted some Radial Reuse land for expansion and that it wasn't about to cooperate with the city in redeveloping the area for a park and residential uses," noted Topher Hansen, another of Malone's neighborhood leaders.

"The university didn't say 'Screw you,' " Hansen said with more than a trace of bitterness in his voice. "They just said 'We're moving in, like it or lump it.' But that's when the neighborhood decided to say 'Screw you' back to them. That's when we forced the power play."

The power play, as it turned out, was yet another broad-based committee, complete with tortuous negotiations that took sixteen months to wend their way to a final conclusion in 1988. It started in 1987, when the city set up the Malone Redevelopment Study Committee—made up of neighborhood, city, and university representatives—to try to smooth over the differences between the updated University Comprehensive Facilities Plan and the previously approved, but now university-rejected, Radial Reuse Plan.

The agreement finally reached in 1988 created a six-acre, L-shaped, city-owned park in Malone plus parcels of land targeted for affordable housing development. The university, meanwhile, agreed to expand in three phases, using the future Malone portion of the bike path and linear park as a firm buffer between its eastern boundary and the neighborhood. It was the first time the university had, in effect, signed a "contract" limiting its future expansion. The city council voted unanimously to support the plan, which had also passed muster with the university Board of Regents, the Malone Neighborhood Association, the Malone Community Center, and the Northeast Radial Reuse Task Force.

"The goal was to achieve a plan through consensus," said Diane Morgan, one of the Lincoln community development staffers involved in the process. "Ultimately, that made it a better plan and everyone took a piece of ownership." Morgan said the city's role in the negotiations was as a mediator between the neighborhood and the university. Once the university and Malone's residents buried the hatchet, the city finally produced a long-awaited redevelopment plan for Malone. It was approved early in 1989. Said Hansen, a few months later:

> Ultimately you get a lot more out of it by doing it the way we did than just going to war with each other. Consensus building is all good and well if you have the time and the energy to do it. But a dictatorship might be a hell of a lot easier.

With time, patience, and money running short and a desire on the part of the city to finally get the Malone redevelopment on the fast track, the city declared Malone a "blighted" neighborhood. That made it eligible for tax increment financing (TIF), a mechanism that allows Lincoln to borrow money based on future increases in property tax revenue that it expects within the TIF district. The debt will be repaid through the increased tax money.

So, on an unusually warm winter day in February 1990, we found Lincoln still going about the task of assembling the park site. It was sorting out city-owned land and trying to acquire the rest of the property it needed that was still in private hands. To an outsider, Malone still had the air of a neighborhood in serious trouble. To Lincolnites, however, the neighborhood's potential was more apparent than it had been for a generation or longer.

There remained, though, a kernel of concern that the saga of Malone might not be quite finished. Many residents said that the power relationship between the university and Malone has been permanently altered. Privately, some residents were expressing fear that the University of Nebraska would still renege on the agreement if it decided it really wanted to expand beyond the negotiated boundaries. There was fear the university would have the bigger political clout, should push come to shove. Though against that, some argued that the negotiations received so much attention locally that the university-neighborhood agreement was nearly ironclad.

Dallas McGee, the city official who sweated out years of tough negotiations and then did the hard nuts-and-bolts work of making sure Clinton, Malone, and University Place got put back together again, had moved on to other city duties but said he was sanguine that the truce between Lincoln and its domineering university will stick.

As for the Radial Reuse Task Force, it had officially gone out of business yet still existed in an informal "monitoring" role, ready to spring back into action if one of the neighborhoods got into serious trouble.

Back in Malone, Greg Newport, the house renovating architect and neighborhood leader, said his neighborhood was still walking a very fine line:

> The stigma attached to Malone goes back thirty years. You can't remove that kind of stigma just by talking. There has to be action and that action is rebuilding the neighborhood. Right now it's like a teeter-totter. Anything can send the neighborhood back into the depths of despair. It will be a few years before people say Malone is on solid ground.

Can and will Americans, in city and neighborhood, stick with the "saving" of a neighborhood as long as a bureaucracy may ignore it? It is a question on which Lincoln—sturdy prairie state capital, embodiment of the American heartland—seems to provide, at once, reassurance and everlasting question.

## *Commentary: Lincoln*

ROBERT SHIBLEY: This chapter presents Lincoln's problem as one of vanquishing the highway monster, but at its heart, the project was not about bringing powerful adversaries to their knees. It's not even about the victory of incrementalism over comprehensive planning. It's about the democratic project in its most fundamental sense. The growth of the Neighborhood Alliance, the election of Mayor Helen Boosalis, the redistricting of the city, the transformation of the town from one that had been represented by the "Men's Club" to one where you can't get on the city council without grassroots support—all this is the story of how a place takes hold of its own destiny.

Those changes happened over a twenty-year period. One of the strong vehicles was the effort at comprehensive planning for transportation. It ultimately led to neighborhood reidentification, a reassertion of power, and a coalition of neighborhoods asking "What's important here? Where are we headed?"

**MARY DECKER:** Maybe I am more cynical than most, but don't all projects claim their process was highly democratic? People tend to reinvent history. Nearly every neighborhood has one of these organizations but their impact is always debatable.

**SHIBLEY:** That's what sets this project apart. Many can claim it but few can point to it happening. There was no Neighborhood Alliance—there is now. Helen Boosalis wasn't mayor—she became mayor on a grass-roots platform that was quite unusual for Lincoln. They redistricted. They elected a neighborhood activist to the city council.

**DECKER:** Maybe our goal in communities is to maintain the creative tension that exists between insiders and outsiders, between those who vote and those who influence. Take Chicago—the so-called city of neighborhoods with aggressive adversarial forces. No matter who is mayor or county board chairman, everyone fights everyone else. There's the powerful independent, nonprofit advocacy structure, there are the grass-roots forces, and there are elected officials and the downtown business interests. This creative tension, many argue, makes the city work.

**SHIBLEY:** This goes back to the ideal of the democratic project, that we build into the system a tension between equity and liberty. Those who have power have the ultimate expression of their liberty. The forces of equity must constantly check those libertine aspirations.

Is there a clear intention to establish winners and losers or is there an intention—as you put it before—to "reinvent history"? Reinventing history is a good thing. Over and over, we must reinvent the history of neighborhood involvement, vitality, and ownership of place so people project themselves into the place and culture they live in. As designers and planners, we are in the business of producing culture. One of the ways we do that is to facilitate dialogue around those creative tensions.

One reinterpretation of history that happens all the time is when you set up a situation as win versus lose. You fight like cats and dogs, and then you rewrite the history so that everybody feels that they won. The transformation from win/lose to win/win is important. It's hard to find people in Lincoln who felt that they had lost.

**DECKER:** The truth in these processes is that there are a few crucial people who do critical things, without whom the project fails. When it's over, you never talk about that. You pretend, sitting in that committee meeting, that everyone was equally important, but it's not the truth. If you wish to repeat the process, you have to create the fiction that everyone had a nearly equal role. It's part of the rewriting that makes it possible for new leaders to be born.

**SHIBLEY:** There happened to be many critical people in Lincoln. Each neighborhood had more than one key player who just kept pushing. It's hard to point to only one person who hung on and made it happen. That's encouraging. Maybe it is possible for many people to give a little rather than one person giving their whole life. Also, two or three key players in the planning office gave continuity to the radial plan. The unsung heroes of this story are the civil servants who chose not to be threatened by the rise of the neighborhoods, who in fact created a place for neighborhood involvement and in a very quiet but deliberate way stayed open to that input and facilitated it over two decades.

**DECKER:** One makes a choice in writing up such a story to feature empowerment or leadership, but very often the same story can be written in different ways with an equal amount of truth.

**SHIBLEY:** Well said. And the next question is: What is it about leadership that can become empowering? Lincoln wasn't making a choice between strong leadership on the one hand and empowerment on the other. The leadership that emerged understood their task to be a leadership of community empowerment.

**DECKER:** This story is, in part, a victory of incrementalism over comprehensive planning. It's time to admit that the comprehensive planning approach of some cities doesn't work. People with a planning education tend to come to problems and say, "We need to be comprehensive—anything less is second-rate." But comprehensive planning shouldn't always be a paramount value. Lincoln's approach was more strategic than comprehensive.

You said earlier that we learned in Lincoln that overall vision can still have room for rather spontaneous incremental decisions. I think that by describing it that way, you are endorsing comprehensive planning, saying that it can be improved by making room for spontaneity.

**SHIBLEY:** I don't mean to say it that way. I am interested in the dialogue between the small acts and a comprehensive vision where neither enjoys power over the other. I worry about the tyranny of a totalizing vision but I also worry about the tyranny of always being subject to serendipity.

**DECKER:** City planning is most successful when one is free to amend and depart from the plan. Even though the vision is orderly, you must be able to say, "This doesn't work." You can't be rigid.

**SHIBLEY:** There's a very strong literature supporting that kind of thinking, but it is not for just any end that we engage in planning. There is a vision. The question is: What's the vision? We can't be relativists. We have to take a position and then be ready to negotiate.

**DECKER:** We idealize two opposing ideas in planning in the twentieth century. One is empowerment and local decision making, but in the Stowe chapter, we note that our favorite cities are Haussmann's Paris or the Ringstrasse of Vienna. Robert Moses is vilified for his process while thousands enjoy the things he built.

Speaking of Robert Moses, it may be worth adding something about transportation planning. It is the toughest kind of planning. It tends to be people versus technology, blood and sweat versus steel and rubber. The transportation planners are always the bad guys and those who fight them are always the good guys. Transportation planners often make the mistake of not allowing for their fallibility. There's an assumption that their work is precise, the product of a technical discipline, so their plans are presented as fact, independent of values and local decisions.

**SHIBLEY:** There's a quote from Moses that I like a lot but it terrifies me: "If the ends don't justify the means, then what the hell does?" This is the so-called bold, courageous planning stroke, as if it's not possible to take bold strokes in the public interest *with* the public. The choice appears to be: either we're going to have to live with the incrementalism of public involvement or we're going to be able to have a real utopian vision with a strong individual to make it happen.

I disagree. That choice says that ends and means cannot be separated. Both choices are about a community's relationship to place. The vision driving the Radial Reuse plan was to help the community put itself back in touch with a neglected notion of itself. It is neither a vision of means nor a vision of ends per se. The vision is about the relationship between means and ends.

**DECKER:** You can't separate the physical place from the human process. Physical places can be powerful motivating forces. Physical visions become transcendent values for the community. Chicago, a town known for political infighting and building huge edifices, has always amazed me with the extent to which it holds its lakefront sacred. Unlikely and exhilarating coalitions form when the lakefront is threatened. It's a shared public vision.

**SHIBLEY:** In Lincoln, a fairly modest ribbon of highway, a bicycle path, and a few parks set in motion a series of events that reinvested Lincoln with an idealistic vision of what a city can be.

CHAPTER 5

# *Farm Workers' Own Housing: Self-Help in Cabrillo Village*

Endless groves of lemon trees. Fertile farmland, glowing lush green with strawberry and tomato plants, resounding with the clack, clack, clack of irrigation equipment bringing water to parched soil. Towering mountains, colored desert brown, cradling some of the world's most productive land. Freeways threading snakelike over the face of the land, filled at every hour with cars and people on their way to somewhere. Continent's end. The edge of America. The pounding, rough turquoise surf of the Pacific.

This is Ventura County, nestled along the Southern California coast, some eighty miles due north of Los Angeles. It is a backwater, really, of the sprawling, thriving City of Angels, hidden southward behind the barrier of the Santa Monica Mountains.

You feel the pulse of the American dream here, especially on radiant days when the sun shines purely and the haze and smog burn off to reveal the mountains, an azure blue sky, the breathtaking vistas, the towering rows of palms, the man-made landscape blooming on territory that would otherwise be bone-dry. Here is a magnet luring busloads of newcomers twenty-four hours a day, 365 days a year, with the promise that someday *they too* might realize their dreams.

At such times, it is easy to forget the brooding cloud; to ignore the fact that Southern California is also becoming our national warning beacon: that the land of honey is turning into a place where gangs of bored, alienated teenagers infest city and suburb alike; that Americans' Promised Land of milk and honey has become a mind-boggling agglomeration of traffic and senseless sprawl; that here is the land that contributed the drive-in restaurant *and* the drive-by shooting to the American psyche; a place where the air is usually so filthy that murky skies are taken for granted; where buying a home—not a big mansion occupied by Hollywood stars but just a little place the average person can call home—defies the budget of ordinary citizens.

This schizophrenia hits one hard in Ventura, as strongly as anywhere else in the Golden State. This is neither farm country nor big city nor even suburb. It is neither the exclusive province of wealthy Anglos nor the shabby home of struggling Mexican immigrants who tend the fields and call this place El Norte. Many of the boulevards have proper Anglo names, such as Harbor and Main and Seaward, but a lot of the streets have Spanish names, such as Arroyo and Baja. It is a resort town that fills on weekends to the breaking point with blond-haired boys and girls catching a tan. Yet its workaday roots are too close to the surface for one to think of this as a Palm Springs or a San Clemente. While agriculture is Ventura's lifeblood, the subdivisions seem to go up faster than the tomatoes ripen on the vine. Farmers are called "growers" here, yet the last crop the growers usually bring in is houses. The professionals who live in Ventura's suburban ramblers routinely shell out $300,000 and $400,000 for the privilege (and those prices of the early 1990s reflected a 25 percent *deflation* in value as the hyperinflated California real estate market softened). The farm workers who form the backbone of the Ventura economy, however, work for some of the lowest wages in the nation.

This land north of Los Angeles can seem timeless. In a car cruising up the Pacific Coast Highway, winding around the hairpin turns that lead from Malibu to Point Magu (a majestic rock that juts defiantly into the Pacific), all one need do is throw on a Beach Boys tape to make everything feel like the 1960s again.

Then, quite suddenly, the coastline disappears and the coastal highway veers inland, slicing through the fields and past the buildings where oranges, lemons, lettuce, and the other produce grown on these lands are warehoused, waiting to be shipped around the nation. Out across the fields, one sees bands of immigrant laborers hunched over, picking strawberries and other produce by hand, figures transposed as if in a time warp from the Okies of *The Grapes of Wrath.*

Then one's car gets caught in the traffic of Oxnard, a town grimly industrial in places, where discount tire and clothing stores line the road and their backsides face vast fields. Here and there, the landscape is broken by huge food storage warehouses and processing plants. Then, finally, one is upon Ventura and its *salsa* of farms and subdivisions.

Cabrillo Village occupies twenty-five acres of land on the edges of Saticoy, a little farm town, situated between Ventura and Oxnard, a neighborhood where agribusiness names such as Dole adorn many buildings and the streets often rumble with the sound of the tractor and tractor-trailer. To get to Cabrillo Village, you turn off the road connecting Saticoy with Ventura and bounce a short distance down a side road until you get to a sleepy little cluster of homes and stores. Cabrillo sits at the end of a dead-end road next to the Santa Clara River, a typical Southern California stream that has a channel but no water. There is one way in and one way out. Pastoral-looking lemon groves surround the village on three sides. On the fourth sits a railroad spur and a subdivision of recent vintage.

Late in the afternoon, the sounds of screaming, squealing children echo through the narrow residential streets of Cabrillo. They are kicking balls along Cinco de Mayo Street (named for the Mexican Independence Day). They are hanging off the jungle gym in the little playground set near the entrance to the community. A bunch of teenage boys are going at it on the village soccer field. The smell of Mexican food wafts out of countless kitchens. It is nearly dinnertime. A few people are tinkering with their cars, some of them junks and some expensive new imports. Some older kids—maybe of legal age, maybe not—are in an out-of-the-way corner downing a few beers, killing time next to an old wreck up on cinder blocks. "We gotta get out of this chickenshit town," one of them laughs.

It is hard to imagine that this community of 160 new and renovated homes used to be a place where farm workers survived life in squalid housing owned by the growers who employed them. Cabrillo began life as a farm workers' camp, with dormitories, warehouses, and a company store. It was built in 1936 by the local lemon growers, planned for single men who followed the harvest north and came to pick the fruit off the trees. There were originally about one hundred worker cabins on the site. Most of them were tiny, less than five hundred square feet each. The streets were unpaved. What began as dormitory housing for single men slowly evolved into cramped homes for large families as many of the single workers married and took up permanent residence in the camp. The population quadrupled beyond what the housing was built to handle.

By anyone's standards, Cabrillo Village was a miserable place. The houses had single walls that left the houses freezing in cold weather. Plumbing was a toilet and a kitchen sink. The sewerage system for the houses emptied into two open settling ponds near the dry riverbed, with the result that when the wind was right, the entire camp had an aroma normally associated with Third World shanty-

***The old Cabrillo. What began as dormitory housing for single men slowly evolved into cramped homes for large families.*** *(Photograph courtesy of Tim Street-Porter, Hollywood, California)*

towns. To top it all off, the settlement was surrounded by a chain-link fence topped with barbed wire.

Cabrillo's residents remember the old days with nary a touch of nostalgia. We encountered Fidel and Amparo Martinez, residents of Cabrillo Village since 1968, sitting in the neat living room of their renovated home decorated with pictures of three of their children—a California Highway Patrol officer, a local police officer, and a firefighter. A big-screen TV silently displayed news coverage of America's latest entanglement in the Mideast—the crisis in Iraq. As his wife sat next to him knitting, Martinez remembered what life in his home used to be like. His wife gave him a knowing look as he began to speak. "It was deplorable," he said. "The house was half the size it is now. It was very cold at night because we had single walls with cracks in them, and it was very crowded."

## *Birth of a Movement*

In 1974, the nation was just becoming aware of the plight of immigrant farm workers in California. A man named Cesar Chavez—the

Mexican-American activist whose struggle to unionize farm workers and humanize their brutal working and living conditions caught the attention of a nation—was making the jump from California newspapers into headlines coast to coast. The farm economy was changing radically as well. The global marketplace was developing and growers in California—and farmers around the nation—were starting to watch their profits shrink after a long period of relatively good times. At Cabrillo Village, many of the formerly transient immigrants had become permanent residents and workers. The growers deducted their rent (about $1.50 a week) from their checks.

The same labor unrest that had hit the great inland agricultural valleys of California was about to come home to roost in Ventura County. In October 1974, Cabrillo's farm laborers walked out on the local lemon growers, demanding higher wages and better working conditions. Several of the leaders of the action fanned out to labor camps around the county, trying to organize strikes by hundreds of other farm workers. The job action by Cabrillo's workers lasted for a tense month before the growers acceded to the workers' demands and signed a settlement. It included wage increases and promises of improved working conditions. The growers, however, proceeded to ignore many of the settlement terms, and so, the following month, the workers began a second organizing drive, this time under the auspices of Chavez's ornery United Farm Workers union, the UFW. The strike proved to be the first step in a chain of events leading not only to the organization of the workers but to the confrontations that would lead to the rebuilding of Cabrillo Village.

An election was scheduled for August 1975 to certify the UFW. A few weeks before the scheduled vote, hoping to forestall the vote, the growers fired 190 workers. Not only did the certification election never take place but six weeks later all of Cabrillo's residents received eviction notices. The families were given thirty days to leave the camp and were offered $500 for relocation expenses—an amount that did not go far in Ventura County, even before the real estate boom of the 1980s began to raise housing prices beyond the reach of all but the most affluent residents. The growers said they had no choice. The camp needed to be razed because of a huge number of health and safety violations—some 1,600 of them—that California housing inspectors had uncovered. Among other things, the village needed a new sewer system and all the homes required completely new plumbing and electrical wiring. The state had also ordered the growers to put the cabins on concrete foundations. The renovations, the bulk of which resulted from decades of neglect by the camp's owners, would have cost millions of dollars, but on top of that, residents detected a more sinister motive at work: the local growers were trying to quash the union organizing activities by dispersing the workers. Similar tactics had been used successfully to hamper organizing efforts around California.

At first, Cabrillo's residents reacted with fear. In the words of Jesus Macias, who moved to California as a farm worker in 1962 and took up residence in Cabrillo in 1972:

> There was tremendous anxiety that the community would cease to exist. We didn't know what would happen. I had a big family. The salary was low. Most of us had nowhere to go. There was a feeling of loneliness and fright, especially the fear that we would end up homeless.

Then Cabrillo's people began to fight back. Chavez and other UFW leaders counseled them to stay put. Inspired by that word, the workers began to enlist the support of activists throughout the county and around the state. They pressured the governor—liberal Democrat Jerry Brown at the time—to put off the eviction so the residents could buy time to come up with alternatives. Brown and his associates were sympathetic to the farm worker movement. The political pressure exerted by Brown and others, in turn, won Cabrillo's residents several stays of eviction from the growers.

Fifteen years later, we visited Jose Campa, a strapping farm worker turned auto mechanic, in his Cabrillo Village home. Campa was dressed in navy blue work overalls and old brown work boots, shoes that told of hard work with worn leather. His thick hands were covered with grime and grease from working on the car in the driveway of his front yard, a spot presided over by two noisy cockatoos. Campa recalled the struggle to organize the union and keep Cabrillo from tumbling before the growers' bulldozers. He reached into his wallet and proudly produced an old union card, one of the first ones issued in 1975 by the UFW. Campa, who came to the United States in 1957 and moved to Cabrillo in 1965, remembered the collective spirit of the 1970s as though the events had taken place only weeks earlier:

> Chavez and the union gave us courage. He told us to take courage in unity, that if we were evicted not to disperse. There was safety in numbers. In the many there was an opportunity for triumph.

As it turned out, many of the most activist of the farm workers in the clash with the growers would soon emerge as the leaders of the movement to preserve Cabrillo Village. One of them was Luis Magdalleno, who was described by Dewey Bandy, an associate at the Center for Cooperatives at the University of California at Davis (who studied Cabrillo in 1990), as

> a cool, level-headed leader. His articulate, reasoned manner of public speaking was complemented with a keen analytic mind. He was highly respected in the village for his intelligence, integrity, and objectivity. Like other key leaders who were to follow him, Luis had a strong commitment to democracy and consensus. His style was to transform the aspirations and goals of the people into a workable plan of action.

Most Cabrillo families realized their only acceptable option was to fight, to fight hard, to fight to save the homes that many of them had been occupying for ten to twenty years. Under the guidance of such leaders as Magdalleno, they persevered, winning outside support and, finally, widespread media attention. There were protests. Children and teenagers marched for miles. All-night vigils were held at the homes of the growers. The UFW offered Cabrillo's residents training in leadership and empowerment. The Catholic church not only provided the village church for meetings but it sent a priest from its Migrant Ministry. He was the first person to suggest the workers buy their homes from the growers.

Discovering the growers had actually signed an option to sell a private buyer the entire village for $80,000, the workers shifted gears and began a letter-writing and picketing campaign that eventually convinced the potential new owner to abandon his plans.

Then the growers escalated the struggle. One day, bulldozers appeared, ready to level the former homes of the few workers who had decided to take the $500 in relocation money and leave. A classic standoff ensued. The residents linked arms and formed a "human circle" around the building that bulldozers had come to flatten. It was a pivotal moment in the struggle, one of those events tailor-made for the TV cameras, an opportunity to galvanize broad public support. Stopping the bulldozers was probably the single incident that turned the tide irrevocably toward the residents' favor.

Campa's narrative vividly illustrated the drama of the confrontation and how close to tragedy the situation actually came:

> The growers came to scare the hell out of us with bulldozers to demolish the houses. After the first house was demolished, the families formed a human chain around the next one and the union representative stood there and told the bulldozer operator that he'd be responsible if anything happened to us. The police arrived, about sixteen cars. At that time, police intimidation had worked elsewhere. But here, they didn't harm anyone. They backed off because too many people were watching. I am certain that if the police had harmed anyone they would have been harmed. There were people in the community who were armed and ready to defend themselves.

In the six months that followed, the workers organized into a corporation, elected a board of directors, and began meeting with the Saticoy Growers Association, seeking to negotiate a purchase price for the camp. Aid came in many forms and from different camps: from the UFW, the Catholic church, the church-sponsored Campaign for Human Development, Self-Help Enterprises (a Quaker-sponsored group), and from a man named Rodney Fernandez. The director of human relations for Ventura County at the time, Fernandez would later go to work directly for the Cabrillo residents, guide the rebuilding of the village through its most crucial phases, and then emerge as an advocate for low-income farm workers throughout Ventura County.

After months of hard-nosed bargaining, the residents and the lemon growers agreed on an $80,000 sale price for the entire labor camp—precisely the amount the private buyer had been willing to invest.

## *Realizing the Victory*

Negotiating an agreement with the growers was contentious, but getting the residents to agree on a game plan was equally sticky. For their part, Cabrillo's residents had to determine what form of ownership they wanted. The majority voted to form a nonprofit corporation, but twenty families declined and organized as a separate for-profit group that made a competing offer to the growers to purchase the camp. Ultimately, the growers accepted the offer of the nonprofit group—the Cabrillo Improvement Association. On May 5, 1976 (Cinco de Mayo), Cabrillo's residents took ownership of the property. The dissenting families, called "the Twenty" by the other residents, continued to fight. The feud with the Twenty was eventually settled by Cabrillo's board of directors and the dissident families joined the nonprofit association. While the Twenty finally became members of the association in 1979, it would be years before the hostilities generated by the internal conflict began to subside.

Along the way, Cabrillo's residents faced a number of obstacles, stumbling blocks that could have tripped them up and ended the dream of rebuilding the village. The first challenge was raising the $80,000 they needed to buy the labor camp. The task was all the more difficult because the so-called Twenty were pursuing their own independent strategy. To buy the project, each family had to invest $1,000. Lacking investment from the twenty dissident families, however, the organizers came up short of cash. Some of the families were well enough off to put more money into the project and did. The UFW stepped in with loans to fill the rest of the gap. Eventually, the workers secured a loan from the Housing Assistance Council that allowed them to pay back the UFW and the residents who had put in more than $1,000. The families were assessed $16.33 a month to repay the loan.

There were also showdowns about how to structure the development. The residents had a choice: they could form a limited equity co-op (the route advocated by Chavez and the other UFW leaders) or they could build a subdivision that would be developed on a for-profit basis. As it turned out, Ventura County zoning ordinances effectively barred development of a subdivision because of the village's seriously deteriorated infrastructure. It was unlikely the residents could raise enough money to do the repairs the county regulations would have required for a subdivision. There was an even more sizable obstacle blocking the for-profit route, however: as a money-making venture, Cabrillo would not qualify for grants and other financial assistance. In the end, the resident settled on rebuilding Cabrillo Village as a cooperative.

Fernandez, who saw Cabrillo grow from an organizers' dream to a living organism, recalled some of the difficulties:

> It was rough because this was a totally foreign experience to the residents. They had the vision and they had the leadership, but not the experience. A lot of the early years were spent getting comfortable with self-management and making decisions even though there was dissension. Dealing with the dissension and the learning process were the hardest things. The project was blessed with strong leaders. But there were still really trying times as everybody learned how to live out their new roles. Relatively speaking, the development part was easy.

Even after they agreed on how to proceed, the residents still had to find a way to make Cabrillo Village habitable. The money required was far beyond what it had cost them to buy the labor camp. What followed was a long process of fund-raising that ultimately opened the gates to large amounts of public money and foundation grants. The California Department of Housing and Community Development took the first step, providing $12,000 for the fledgling co-op to do a housing feasibility study and determine both the renovation needs and cost. Six months later, the Campaign for Human Development granted the co-op $100,000 to hire a coordinator for a year and make the necessary hookups to Ventura's water and sewerage systems. Ventura County kicked in money for road improvements.

Financing the rehabilitation of the existing cottages—many of which would be more than doubled in size, from 500 square feet to 1,200 square feet—was not an easy task. In 1978, Cabrillo received a $13,000 grant from the Rosenberg Foundation for a pilot project.

The residents would renovate one home using one paid supervisor and volunteers from the village. Self-Help Enterprises, the Quaker group, which had experience in developing rural housing, provided technical assistance for the demonstration project. The experiment worked, producing a simple yet very habitable home lacking in many of the "frills" later residences were to have.

With the first home complete and some tangible proof that the residents of Cabrillo were up to the challenge of rebuilding the village, the California housing department awarded the community $216,000 for equipment and material for fourteen more homes. Cabrillo's residents were lucky in more ways than one: their timing was crucial. This was the late 1970s, and the government money, from an array of programs, was still available. Only a few years later, in the early 1980s, the flow of federal funds would dry to a trickle and then virtually evaporate—at the same time that California coffers were drying up in the wake of the tax-slashing Proposition 13 passed by voters in 1978. Residents obtained job training money, for instance, from the Comprehensive Employment and Training Act, the much-maligned federal jobs program that expired during the first round of Reagan-era budget cuts of the early 1980s. The federal job training money allowed the village to set up four work crews of residents; a local community college provided on-the-job training as the renovation work went forward. Almost all of the laborers on the project were farm workers. The vast majority became skilled in a variety of trades, from carpentry to plumbing to electrical work. Many were made able to trade in their jobs as farm workers for higher paying craftsmen jobs after the Cabrillo construction work was completed. Many never returned to working the fields.

By the time the Cabrillo project was finally completed, the residents had received public and private development financing totaling $7.94 million. The government money came from a panoply of programs: Nearly $4 million was provided by the Farmers Home Administration (FmHA), a government lender that rarely provided financing for cooperatives and in fact had its origins in assisting farmers and growers, not farm workers. California's Department of Housing and Community Development provided a total of $1.2 million. Nearly $1 million came from the federal Community Development Block Grant and Comprehensive Employment Training Act programs. Another $400,000 was provided by the federal Economic Development Administration, an agency that would be slimmed down to near invisibility as the Reagan-era proceeded.

The private sector and foundations also participated heavily in the Cabrillo undertaking: More than $200,000 in loans were provided by private lenders. The Campaign for Human Development and Rural America each contributed $230,000. The Rosenberg Foundation provided $175,000.

Another forty-six homes were renovated through 1980. Work proceeded at a pace of eight to ten homes per year (progress slowed as government money became less and less available) until all of the work was finally completed in 1986. The renovation work on the old cabins was extensive. New foundations were laid. Floors were replaced. Walls were insulated and finished on the insides of the homes. The exteriors of many homes received stucco finishes. New bathrooms, kitchens, and electrical and plumbing systems were installed. In most cases, the homes were expanded to add desperately needed bedroom space. Whenever possible, materials were salvaged and reused. Many of the fences in the village, for example, were built from siding removed from the old cottages.

As the old cottages in the village were slowly renovated and rebuilt, the co-op set out to add new housing on empty land at the edge of Cabrillo. One complex of town houses, thirty-five homes in all, was finished in 1981. Another complex of thirty-nine homes started construction in 1983. The Cabrillo homes built from scratch still displayed the sensitivities that the architects hired by the co-op had brought to the project. The designers did not have an easy charge. They were forced to walk a tightrope between the FmHA's bagful of regulations and the desires of residents, who had put much of their own thought and enthusiasm into the design of the new housing. By 1990, the buildings were starting to show signs of wear—front yards that were not kept up, paint that was needed here and there, solar panels that desperately cried out for a washing. Yet it was still remarkably hard to detect that these homes were, in fact, low-income housing. Cabrillo's new homes were light years from the stereotype of the grim, government-financed housing built to warehouse the poor.

The sensitive architecture of the new housing, which won kudos from *Time* magazine and several architectural awards, was the handiwork of two Los Angeles designers hired in 1977. The two, John Mutlow, an architect, and Frank Villalobos, a landscape architect, set about designing the housing with a process virtually unheard of in building low-income housing. They held weekly meetings with the community and wrote up a "space use questionnaire" to find out what preferences families had about the interiors of their homes. Residents' desires in large measure determined the housing's design.

As Dewey Bandy wrote in his study of Cabrillo Village:

> The participatory, grass-roots style of Cabrillo Village constituted the foundation of this planning and development process. Residents played an

***Cabrillo's new homes are light years from the stereotype of grim, government-financed housing built to warehouse the poor.*** *(Photograph courtesy of Tim Street-Porter, Hollywood, California)*

active role in formulating goals, weighing options, developing plans, and physically designing the rehabilitation of the village and the cottages.

Residents were given so much of a say in designing the new housing, in fact, that the architects ran head on into the requirements of the FmHA. The residents wanted single-family houses. The FmHA required multifamily town houses. Architect Mutlow came up with a compromise allowing the community to build units that resembled single-family homes in layout, even though they were technically attached. The residents were concerned about how they would be able to pay utilities on their meager farm incomes, so Mutlow worked with them to win a grant from the Department of Housing and Urban Development to install solar energy panels. By using active hot water heating and passive solar space heating, residents were able to save nearly 70 percent on their utility bills.

When the time came to design the second complex of new

***Residents wanted single-family houses but government regulations required attached town houses. Smart design yielded a separated feeling.***

*(Photograph courtesy of Tim Street-Porter, Hollywood, California)*

homes, the architects faced even tougher FmHA-imposed design requirements. Residents wanted an area where their children could play under their supervision. The architects provided it by clustering the new units so that there was a shared central courtyard where the children could play safely. As we visited in 1990, on a late summer afternoon when the sun cast a soft orange glow across the courtyard, the space was one of the liveliest in all of Cabrillo Village.

Residents got around other strings that came with federal funds by simply doing the job themselves. Ventura County required new housing to have carports. The FmHA's requirements specifically barred them. The plans left space for carports and the residents built them on their own later. A community building was also planned as part of the second round of new housing construction. FmHA allowed a far smaller facility than the community wanted. The residents raised $40,000 in cash to increase the size of the meeting space and built a community center with a meeting room big enough to seat the entire community, also including a kitchen and a laundry room.

## *The Fruits of Hard Work*

Rodney Fernandez and Jesse Ornelas are unassuming and friendly but intense men. Both of them are slightly built. Fernandez is the more soft-spoken of the two but is far from quiet. Ornelas is more of a showman, a man who enjoys showing he is in charge, that he has a handle on things. Fernandez is more the quiet planner. Ornelas is the aspiring local politician. Together, they have helped guide the projects and built the organization that are bright spots in the struggle of Ventura County's working poor and working class.

Both Fernandez and Ornelas earned their stripes in the struggle to rebuild Cabrillo Village. By 1990, both had moved on to become prominent advocates for the low-income Mexican immigrants of Ventura County who found themselves caught in one of the nation's most desperate housing and economic situations. It was a situation exacerbated by Ventura's continued dual identity: an ongoing old rural economy rubbing shoulders with the more affluent, professional economy that blossomed in the 1980s.

Cabrillo Village remained as a model of empowerment on one hand, a reminder of the difficult plight of the working poor on the other. If the 1970s were a decade of struggle, victory, and hope for California's immigrant farm workers, the 1980s proved to be a period of dejection, deflation, and, for many, renewed desperation. The labor union that had scored so many victories in the 1970s, the union that had become a national cause célèbre among liberal activists, fell on hard times. By the late 1970s, the UFW had won contracts with most of the major growers in the Ventura area. As the 1980s came to a close, most of the contracts were gone and many of the workers were back where they had started. Cesar Chavez, the man who had garnered headlines around the country, had disappeared from the press in California and become a nonentity nationally. In Ventura, many of the workers and activists who had worked closely with the labor leader in 1975 virtually scorned him in 1990. When they spoke of Chavez at all, they talked in past tense, using language usually reserved to discuss a close relative who had passed away. Chavez himself struggled to gain a foothold that might allow him to regain a measure of the influence he once held and the suasion he once exercised. He died in 1993.

The virtual demise of the UFW contributed to the tenuous existence of Ventura's farm workers, many teetering more precariously than ever on the edge of poverty. The labor market in the agricultural economy had gotten worse. Once workers had been in short supply. By 1990, the market was flooded with new immigrants willing to work for low wages and no benefits. Meanwhile, the baby boom generation professionals who repaired to Ventura County, hoping to outrun the urban sprawl of Los Angeles, brought high salaries with them. That, in turn, bid up the price of everything from food to houses.

No one had a firm count, but some 18,000 to 22,000 farm workers and their families lived in Ventura County in 1990. Unlike other agricultural strongholds of California, where much of the farm labor population was transient, Ventura's was relatively stable. It was not unusual to find older immigrants who first came north and settled in the county in the 1930s; it was routine to find families that had lived there since the 1950s and 1960s. Most of the farm workers—upward of 90 percent of them, by some estimates—remained desperately poor. Family incomes ranged from $8,000 for families with one wage earner up to $28,000 for large families with two spouses and several children employed in farm work.

Ventura County and its environs had become one of the toughest places in America to be poor. Virtually every city in the county—from the most affluent to the most modest—had a barrio of its own. Tent cities where male farm workers lived in pathetic lean-tos, in virtual, if not actual, homelessness, had sprung up on countless dry riverbeds. Most of the communities in Ventura, as well as the county itself, had passed tough growth control laws restricting housing development—but not the office development that attracted workers and residents. The growth measures virtually ignored the problem that poor and working-class people faced in finding shelter. During the 1980s, for instance, 4,500 units of housing had been built in Oxnard. A total of forty-three were low-income units. Many families in the county got by by "doubling up" and "tripling up," which was what they called it when two and three families shared homes designed to house a single family. When families doubled and tripled in Ventura County, there could be as many as two dozen people living under the same roof.

A "social needs survey" of three hundred leaders, sponsored by the local Ventura Foundation in 1990, found housing ranked as the most urgent of fifty needs in the county. Virtually everyone predicted that the area's housing problem would become more serious during the 1990s.

Normally reserved, Fernandez became agitated when he told us about the lack of progress in housing the poor. He began gesturing with his hands to drive home each point:

> There is a tremendous ignorance of the human and economic consequences of not trying to do anything about the problem and there may even be certain degrees of racism. The policy in many places has been to do as little as possible. But the poor people that no one wants are a big cog in the economy. The logic is that the county needs more housing for the affluent to add to the tax base and improve the image and attract business and industry. That's the logic. But the shortcoming in that line of reasoning is that the most important part of the economic equation are the lower paid workers who are doing the bulk of the work in the community. If there is no place for them to live you either lose them or you can't attract them in the first place. It's gotten so bad now that mid-level workers and managers can't even find a place they can afford to live.

Ornelas, who had waded into local politics and was vying to become a city council member in the smaller community of Santa Paula, painted a bleak picture of the consequences of continued inattention to the plight of residents of modest means:

> The situation is going to get worse. Ventura County is becoming the second least affordable place in California. If we don't address our housing needs we'll have more homelessness. People are doubling and tripling and that creates a burden on the housing stock. Neighbors don't like to live next to an area congested with parking and kids running around everywhere. It will lead to frustration and it will separate people along economic and cultural lines. The children will fall behind in education. They won't have job skills. It will be a burden on the entire society.

Cabrillo Village not only served as a monument of what *could* be in Ventura County and similar areas across California. The group that had spawned the farm workers' lead model of self-sufficiency also became a beacon of hope on an otherwise dark landscape. Fernandez, who had taken over as executive director of the Cabrillo Improvement Association, organized a new nonprofit in 1981, the Cabrillo Economic Development Corporation (CEDC). In addition to searching out development opportunities for Cabrillo and its residents, CEDC was to assist other Ventura County organizations develop affordable housing and community facilities. By 1990, CEDC had developed 477 units of housing scattered in several large projects, and it had several hundred more in various stages of development or actual construction. Fernandez confidently told us he expected CEDC's housing production would exceed one thousand units within several years.

However impressive such numbers—especially for a single, small community development corporation—they also underscored the desperate housing needs in Ventura County. The Cabrillo community development organization remained the *only* such group in all of Ventura County. Of everyone we talked to, Fernandez might have been the most reserved in evaluating the impact a single group could have in the face of the county's skyrocketing demand for affordable housing. He said:

> You have to be realistic. We are talking about a population of 20,000 farm workers that needs to be housed. How many of them can we adequately house ourselves? We certainly have the ability to keep doing our share and you will see more low-income people getting into decent housing. Still, our ability to take care of a significant share of the market is limited. The marketplace has to take 90 percent of it.

Whether the marketplace was up to the task remained one of the critical questions confronting not only Ventura but countless other counties around the Golden State. Still, the accomplishments of CEDC stood out as a model of what could be achieved even in the face of incredible adversity. One indicator of the possible was Rancho Sespe, a farm worker housing project that stood as a sudden break in the citrus groves some twenty miles distant from Cabrillo Village. This one hundred-unit project for low-income farm laborers and their families took its name from a huge local ranch that was sold to national agribusiness interests in the 1970s. The struggle by some ninety families to build a Rancho Sespe housing development became one of the most contentious in the nation, a project that almost made rebuilding Cabrillo Village seem like a harmonious, simple affair.

The new agribusiness owners of Rancho Sespe—a group Fernandez angrily called "a new breed of farmer who is callous and inhumane"—followed the Cabrillo model of serving eviction notices on tenants who were trying to form a union. Some of the workers had been living on the ranch for forty years. The legal fight that developed dragged on for eight years. In the process, the case was taken all the way to the U.S. Supreme Court and became the longest eviction battle ever fought in the United States.

Building on the Cabrillo experience, Sespe's residents promptly filed suit alleging that they were being evicted due to their union organizing activities. Even though the courts barred the evictions, the landowners embarked on a concerted war of attrition aimed at making life so intolerable that the workers would leave their homes of their own volition. The water was cut off. Sewerage services were shut down. Gas lines were cut, as was electricity. The residents fought back. They made repairs to keep some water flowing. They brought in bottled propane gas for heating water and cooking. The courts ordered the owners to turn the electricity back on.

Finally, the California Supreme Court—dominated until the mid-1980s by a group of liberal justices who were later ousted by voters—ruled the village would continue to stand and that the workers could stay until suitable replacement housing was found. The landowners appealed to the U.S. Supreme Court, which refused to rule in the case, letting the California Supreme Court's ruling stand. The task force set up by the California state government recommended buying new land for the replacement homes and that $500,000 be made available for a land purchase and improvements to a new site.

That, however, was not the final shot fired in the battle. After several abortive efforts, the residents and CEDC found a suitable site, which was sold to them by a farmer from nearby Santa Barbara who was retiring. Owners of land adjacent to the newly purchased site filed a suit of their own, objecting to the new development. They charged it did not follow county development guidelines because it would remove several acres of agricultural land from production. The courts turned down these objections as well. FmHA provided about $3.5 million to build the project. "The growers wouldn't go for the project because their long-term interests are building subdivisions," Ornelas said as he drove a pickup truck through the curving mountain roads where earthquake faults appeared as sudden dips and inclines in the road that led to the new Rancho Sespe development. "They didn't want farm worker housing in the middle of their twenty-acre subdivision."

Construction finally began in early 1989. The first of the ninety families that had stuck out the long eviction battle moved into fifty Rancho Sespe units that opened in early 1990. By 1992, CEDC hoped to complete another fifty units, a child-care center, and a community center on the site.

## *Epilogue*

As we approached the entrance to Cabrillo Village, a man named Juan Gomez, one of the leaders in the fight to save this place for its people, stood with a half dozen young boys applying white paint to graffiti marring the wall of a building. When Cabrillo opened, the whitewashed wall was a one-hundred-foot folk art mural painted by residents depicting the struggle to save their community. Village teenagers destroyed the mural with graffiti, resulting in a blank wall periodically covered with more graffiti to greet resident and visitor alike.

In 1990, Cabrillo was beginning to display signs of strain and the wear and tear from its long roller-coaster ride. The destruction of the mural might have been an isolated act of vandalism by village teenagers who had limited recreational opportunities. Certainly compared to urban communities facing difficult quandaries it was insignificant. Still, the mural's loss seemed to symbolize something more ominous: a creeping despondency, almost palpable in the air.

The farm worker movement that had stirred so many spirits now lay deflated and listless. The single-minded direction that deeply impressed any observer of the struggle to build Cabrillo had become a rudderless and rather depressing status quo. The 1980s had witnessed an inspirational rise for many of Cabrillo's residents, dozens of people escaping the world of farm work for other pursuits, young people becoming the first in their family to attend college and broaden their career possibilities. Yet by 1990, all that seemed frozen in its tracks. A ceramic tile factory, which Cabrillo leaders had once pointed to with pride as one example of the economic benefits of the village's renewal, stood sadly shuttered. Residents had hoped to market their tiles, which were used in rebuilding many of the Cabrillo homes, but discovered that making the tiles and selling them outside the village were two differet matters. The factory folded.

It is fair to say that the Cabrillo Village we saw in 1990 raised as many questions as it answered. Physically, most of the project had held up well. Yet something was missing, a perception that was reinforced by nearly everyone we met in a place that still, ironically, continued to serve as an inspiration for everyone who came in contact with it. Fernandez explained part of the puzzle:

> The reach challenge is finding enough local leaders to share the burden of placing themselves in leadership positions. Cabrillo was blessed by having

> a series of leaders over time and that was a tremendous asset. But no one has been able to take the next step and serve as a leader to help the co-op develop the new programs it needs. Nothing has been put together.

Fernandez was referring to needs that virtually everyone connected with Cabrillo Village agreed existed. Many of the residents were concerned that plans to develop programs for the teenagers and other young people of Cabrillo Village were stopped dead in their tracks. Problems were beginning to appear in the form of increasing drug use and drinking by teenagers as well as run-of-the-mill vandalism. The child-care facilities that parents in the community desperately needed were still nowhere on the horizon.

We met Socorro Flaco Eilar, a brilliant young woman of twenty-eight who grew up in Cabrillo Village and participated in the marches, protests, and all-night vigils as a teenager. She had earned a degree from Harvard University and then returned home to manage Cabrillo Village for a time. Eilar's parents were both farm laborers. Her father worked for the local lemon growers for two decades, her mother in the local packing houses.

As she sat cradling her three-month-old son, she compared Cabrillo Village to an adolescent going through a troubled period. The transition period would not be easy, she said. She made special note of the fact that while a large number of her peers had gone to college locally and around the country, there had more lately been a precipitous decrease in the number of youngsters attending college. She added:

> There isn't the same spirit as there was before. But it's like that with any struggle. You spend years and years fighting for something and when you finally achieve it there is bound to be a letdown.

Eilar had firsthand knowledge of some of the troubles Cabrillo Village faced. She was brought on to manage the project after a disastrous period of inept management in the late 1980s. In the job, she addressed a multitude of problems and got people thinking more about the village's needs for the future. She left the management job in early 1990 to have her child. Cabrillo's management situation then took another apparent turn for the worse when the community replaced her with a blond-haired, Spanish-speaking, Anglo Mormon missionary with no experience in running a residential project. When we visited, Cabrillo again seemed to be thrown into a netherworld of uninspired—at best static—management. Some residents were complaining bitterly that the community was stuck in neutral gear or had perhaps even slid into reverse.

Bandy, the University of California associate who studied and wrote about Cabrillo in 1990, was at once circumspect and optimistic in drawing his conclusions:

> The future is, of course, open. Which direction the cooperative will go in is something only time can tell. But whatever the direction, for better or for worse, it will be chosen by the residents instead of a rich Anglo grower or labor contractor. And it will be done by people who have stable roots in a community of affordable, high-quality housing.

There was no question Cabrillo Village would survive. The real question was tougher and infinitely more critical: Could and would Cabrillo Village thrive?

If Cabrillo could recover its former dynamism, it promised to stand as a tiny beacon of hope for the hard-working poor everywhere. In a blinding kind of flash, the Cabrillo Village experience had proven the capacity for brilliance, tenacity, energy, and vision among Americans so often written off by mainstream society. Facing the even tougher economic and social challenges of the 1990s, the Cabrillo movement faced a formidable new test of its mettle, but as great a test faced the greater society: whether it cared enough to learn from the Cabrillo experience, to open new doors to the resources, physical and human, needed to make many more Cabrillo Villages grow and flower.

## *Commentary: Cabrillo Village*

ROBERT SHIBLEY: This chapter presents a melancholy picture of Cabrillo Village in decline, but right off one should say "Hooray!" for what has been done there. Cabrillo Village has been a model for five other camp conversions over the past ten years. Living conditions, even now, are multiple orders of magnitude better than they were before. People moved from one-by-two single shell structures with poor sanitation, where parents felt their kids were unsafe, to a middle-class physical setting. They moved from shacks to homes.

AARON ZARETSKY: As with the other winners of the Rudy Bruner Award, such as New York City's TIL program, the key here was self-help. HUD Secretary Jack Kemp might see self-help as justifying the withdrawal of federal financial responsibility. The TIL and Cabrillo programs show that self-help doesn't mean erasing the necessity for public expenditures. It means self-direction, giving people control over the decisions that affect their lives.

My fear is that as we celebrate self-help, the unfortunate effect will be to support the notion of withdrawing public responsibility.

That view neglects the lessons of both these examples—TIL and Cabrillo—where we are dealing with blacks or Hispanics who for decades have been cut off from education, shut out of the market economy, and subjected to the kind of racism that has prevented them from being able to dream of attaining anything like building a house in Southern California with their own resources.

From the standpoint of public funding, the housing in Cabrillo is an incredible bargain. Each unit is self-contained, solar, and energy efficient but costs less than $50,000. The tile factory, the community hall, and the cost of the CETA [Comprehensive Employment and Training Act] training program are all included in that price. The housing authority in Seattle, Washington, where prices are half what they are in Southern California, is delighted when it's able to build apartment units at $60,000 to $70,000.

SHIBLEY: It's also important to remember that this place received honors from *Progressive Architecture* magazine and was featured in *Architectural Record* for its scale and sensitivity, for an architecture that doesn't look like what it costs. With absolutely minimum funding, it has the character and ambience of a comfortable middle-class residential neighborhood. That's a pretty good success story all by itself.

POLLY WELCH: Self-help has given the Cabrillo Village owners upward mobility. One of the most engaging parts of the "limited equity co-op" is that it recycles that opportunity. If you move out you must sell at a predetermined price that allows another low-income family to become a homeowner. Self-help is not a one-time thing. It has an ongoing impact.

ZARETSKY: The limited equity co-op prevents the first owner from being the only one to benefit from public funding. There's no opportunity to sell at an inflated rate, and that prevents the low-income housing from being lost to high prices. It does allow first owners to get on their feet and make a choice between continuing to live in that housing, built with private and federal assistance, or moving on.

WELCH: Cabrillo Village is a poignant lesson of what happens when a project reaches adolescence. At the time I visited Cabrillo in 1989, none of the co-op units had ever been put on the market. They were transferred from one family member to another. There's a real sense of permanence, but the original residents also clearly have compassion for other people like themselves. This is reflected in their commitment to getting the Farmer's Home housing built, so that other farm workers could have a chance at home ownership.

But there's an interesting twist here, an irony. The original owners sound different from the new arrivals. They speak with great emotion about what the project has done for their lives. The newer residents who bought into the second and third phase don't appear to have the same relationship to the village. They have less emotional investment, less willingness to come to meetings, less awareness of how much energy, time, and participation it takes to keep a cooperative going. The original organizers are having a difficult time finding new, younger board members.

**SHIBLEY:** The life of Cabrillo will go in cycles. Pretty soon someone will decide, for example, that it is not acceptable if fewer kids are going off to college than before. This is a very strong and family-oriented social group, and they will bring it back to life in the vision of a new generation of leaders. Right now they are in that awful in between, an adolescence. They won their first fight and haven't quite figured out what their second fight is, but there are positive signs. If the graffiti on the mural was a sign of the project's decline, the whitewashing is a layer that makes you optimistic about what is going to happen next.

**ZARETSKY:** When you're living in a tar-paper shack with no sewerage, surrounded by barbed wire, your total being is focused on obtaining decent housing. Then there's an excitement around finally achieving it. Once you're living in a reasonable shelter, other realities descend on you. Those people are still isolated from America. In Southern California, you have a steam engine of progress for the material culture. These people are separated from that by lack of education, low wages, racism, the force of history. Having decent housing doesn't solve that. If they are despondent, it's because housing isn't their only problem.

**WELCH:** The story of Cabrillo Village illustrates the tension between mercy and justice. This was mercy funding, as opposed to righting the wrongs. You solve the immediate problem, in this case housing, rather than the larger problems of poor education and healthcare, drugs, much less giving people the services they need to solve family problems and get on with their lives.

The original eighty migrant families were able to use the mercy money to right other wrongs. For the original residents, the very process of creating Cabrillo was an education: people learning about financing, learning the politics of getting things from the county, learning construction skills, learning how to manage. They became very articulate. They learned everything from empowerment to daily skills. Many have gone on to better-paying jobs. They aspire to get their children into college. In contrast, the people who moved into the brand-new units got a nice home rather than a migrant worker camp, but they didn't get the empowerment and self-education that organizing brings.

Another difference between the first and later generations at Cabrillo is in the appearance of the housing itself. Much of the first-phase housing is highly personalized. Residents rebuilt every inch of their homes. Even outside, people inserted tiles into the stucco, set up rose arbors, painted gutters different colors. The later phases of housing are attractive but with less expression of their occupants,

ZARETSKY: Part of the reason they were fixing up their homes has to do with the sense of ownership. It brings a sense of security. You don't fix up what's not yours.

WELCH: The original residents preferred the old housing; when the new housing was built, they chose not to move. The original owners participated in the design discussions for the new units, so the architects assumed that they would want to move in when the units were complete. No one did, to the surprise and disappointment of the architects.

They didn't want to move, in part, because the new homes were attached—not the American dream of the detached home. More importantly, it was because they had made an emotional investment in their first homes. The new homes didn't require that effort. They were complete. Some new homeowners are delighted not to lift a paintbrush, but for a person looking to make a home of her own, putting in that energy is important.

ZARETSKY: The concept of the work ethic is deeply ingrained in our culture. If you work hard you will have the good life. The reality for farm workers is that there is no more backbreaking, hazardous work with longer hours and yet they are totally impoverished. It's ironic that we would celebrate that they would have to build their own houses. It's a model of people going home after sixty to ninety hours of hard work in ninety-five-degree weather to build their own carports.

The story of Cabrillo Village is very much the story of the impact of racism in our culture. "Yankees" willing to work that hard would not be living in tar-paper shacks, building their own homes. They would be earning too much. The residents of Cabrillo Village are not interlopers in a white culture. A hundred and fifty years ago, California and the American Southwest were populated by Mexican people. It's a testament to the impact of racism that they are now seen as outsiders coming in to do the drudgery.

CHAPTER **6**

# *The Stowe Recreation Path: Common Ground*

As sunlight dapples the path before you, Vermont's Stowe Recreation Path offers a mind-boggling variety of human activity.

Everywhere there seem to be joggers, strollers, "power walkers." Cyclists roll by on everything from tricycles to fifteen-speed bikes. Several mothers stroll by pushing baby carriages; one is in her jogging togs, toning up her leg muscles with a high-speed carriage roll.

A middle-aged couple is out for a brisk afternoon walk. A bag lady passes by, collecting whatever she can find. Around the bend comes an octogenarian couple, the elderly gentleman in his wheelchair, his wife pushing him along.

Interspersed with the locals are tourists to Vermont's most famous ski and summer resort. For an hour or two, they have abandoned their automobiles to enjoy a true New England townscape on foot; or in wintertime, oftentimes on cross-country skis.

Most of all, the path seems to draw kids. Kids in strollers. Kids walking. Kids running. Kids on roller skis and roller blades and other contraptions few of us who are over thirty can identify. Little tots, grade-school kids, a high school contingent. Spotted all along the path, kids hanging out at their favorite spots.

Everyone in Stowe seems to have incorporated the recreation path into his or her daily life. This walkway, new in the 1980s, has suddenly become Stowe's new main street, a path for all.

And not just that. The path seems to have given rebirth to old-fashioned American community sociability. On almost every "passing by," eye contact gets made. Words of greetings, or some other friendly gesture, are offered. Sometimes people engage in complete conversations about the weather, the stream, perhaps someone's dog or child. These are not just conversations among friends or acquaintances but between practically anyone on the path—"townie" or tourist, male or female, young or old, blue jean or Abecrombie and Fitch clad.

Here are some basic facts and vital statistics about the Stowe Recreation Path: It is 5.3 miles in length, having been built in two segments—first 2.7 miles, then 2.6 miles—between 1984 and 1989. It consists of an eight-foot-wide asphalt strip laid on a four-inch gravel base with about three feet of grass on each shoulder. It runs from the heart of the village of Stowe, up to the lower flanks of Mount Mansfield, paralleling Stowe's Mountain Road (State Route 108, the main access road to the Mount Mansfield ski area) and the West Branch River. It actually crosses the river ten times by means of ten-foot cambered bridges.

This path is not deluxe, fancy, manicured, or perfect. Along with cameo views of placid Vermont scenes, the route has a reasonable quota of backyards and dumpster views. It is not a fancy creation (the total construction cost was $657,000, small change in the world of modern infrastructure costs). The project did not happen overnight; indeed, between conception of the idea for the path (1977) to completion of the final segment (1989), a dozen years elapsed. The

***The Stowe Recreation Path runs 5.3 miles, from the heart of the village to the lower flanks of Mount Mansfield. The total construction cost was only $657,000.***

*(Photograph courtesy of Jeff Turnau, Stowe, Vermont)*

inspiration of having a path in the first instance came from outside government—so did the major push to get it built.

Whatever the Stowe Recreation Path may lack in English garden-style perfection, in massive case investment, or in foresight by public officials, it more than makes up for it on other fronts. It is an exemplar of enthused citizen initiative. It illustrates shrewd Yankee use of a constrained dollar. It offers, to the eye, a flowing, undulating form, relating naturally, delightfully to the Vermont townscape and mountainscape through which it threads.

## *A Pathway's Origins*

Though the town of Stowe nestles beside Mount Mansfield (at 4,393 feet Vermont's highest peak), tourism was unthought of in its early years. It shared in the state's early wave of settlement as pioneers cleared the land and sold potash from the fallen trees. In the early 1900s, when a million sheep bells could be heard on Vermont's hills, Stowe grazed eight thousand sheep across Mansfield's broad slopes and gentler elevations. Later came a great dairying era, with one hundred Stowe family farms tending 2,800 cows. (The bovine population was almost double the people count of some 1,500 in the 1930s.)

A flow of summer visitors began in the late nineteenth century, and the ski industry got under way in a big way just before World War II. The hills became honeycombed with ski trails, and Stowe declared itself to be the ski capital of eastern America. Some sixty lodges sprang up to tap the wintertime visitor bonanza. In recent years, the summer visitor tide has become practically as heavy. The population has risen to 3,300 permanent residents. One focus of activity is found along Main Street and Stowe Village, but Stowe has also expanded with many homes, restaurants, shops, and offices in the band of territory tucked between the seven-mile road to Mount Mansfield and the West Branch River. The town's elementary and high schools are also nearby.

Claire Lintilhac, who had lived for years near the end of the Mountain Road, became concerned in the late 1970s about the narrow roadway's dangers for walkers and bikers, especially mothers pushing their baby carriages. She expressed her concern to the Vermont Highway Department, commissioning it (anonymously, through a newly founded family foundation) to conduct a $18,000 study on the potential of a bike/pedestrian path connecting Stowe Village and the mountain. Most townspeople felt, however, that the plan the highway planners came up with was too grandiose, so the project remained on hold until 1981, when the Long Range Planning Committee of the Stowe Area Association—the town's Chamber of Commerce—asked the selectmen to include on the town meeting ballot a request for $10,000 to hire a bike path coordinator. The town meeting approved; the idea was to find a willing candidate for the job at a princely $5,000 a year.

## The Lusk Factor

Enter Anne Lusk, the woman who would prove herself not only the visionary and exponent but the planner, the implementor, the champion, and in time the national voice for the Stowe Recreation Path. Lusk had spent a girlhood near Pittsburgh, Pennsylvania, in a set-

***Anne Lusk, the visionary and champion of the Stowe Recreation Path. She persuaded dozens of landowners to donate easements cost-free.*** *(Photograph courtesy of Jeff Turnau, Stowe, Vermont)*

ting—as she would later recall—"of woods, salamander streams, violet fields, and caves to explore." She had attended Ohio University in Athens and had lived at times in Japan and Morocco. A graduate in fashion design from France's Les Ecoles de la Chambre Syndicale de la Couture Parisienne, she had received a master of arts in teaching, specializing in historic preservation, at the University of Vermont in Burlington and taught weaving there. She decided, after working for a while as a fashion model in New York City in the early 1970s, to try out being a Stowe ski bum for a season.

The season would turn out to be a long one (but she was only briefly a ski bum). In Stowe, Lusk met a local tree surgeon who had come there from Connecticut. They married, had two children (a daughter and son), and settled down into normal family life.

Lusk also plunged into local civic activity. Just before the selectmen picked her as path coordinator, she had completed—as a volunteer—a town project to convert the old Stowe school into the town library and art center. Everyone had been impressed by her vigor and persistence in the job. Choosing between a professional planning and engineering firm on the one hand and Lusk on the other, the selectmen cannily figured they would get more for less by picking Lusk. The price of $5,000 a year, for two years, matched anyone's idea of New England frugality.

Lusk is blonde, attractive, dynamic. To an outsider, she seems to have outshone any and everyone else involved with the path, but no fast-talking blonde is going to get the selectmen and other seasoned figures of a New England town—even a sophisticated town like Stowe—to undertake a project as important as the recreation path unless she has taken extraordinary care and thought to lay a foundation, personal and political, with the local establishment.

Lusk's initial task, it would turn out, entailed persuading twenty-seven of Stowe's property owners to donate, *cost-free,* easements for the path's initial 2.7-mile stretch (the first chunk beginning in Stowe Village and starting up the Mountain Road); to raise close to $300,000 through a mixture of local contributions and federal funds; and to reassure selectmen and townspeople alike, at each step, that the Stowe Recreation Path was something they all wanted and would continue to support.

It is instructive to note what Lusk did *not* do in this process.

She did *not* plunge into immediate surveying and construction work on the path nor did she launch an early fund-raising campaign. Instead, she spent a full year publicizing—chiefly through a series of articles in the *Stowe Reporter*—the multiple benefits that could flow to Stowe through a quality path. The project, she emphasized repeatedly, would surely be for recreation but it would accomplish much more—preserve open space, undergird the town's social fabric, provide a method of safe and affordable transportation, and make all parts of the town more accessible to citizens.

By the time the year of publicity was completed, the Stowe Recreation Path had begun to take on an apple pie and motherhood image—a project of potential, multiple benefits for everyone in town.

Lusk did *not* take any early steps that might have been threatening to individual landowners. She laid out no specific, detailed route for the path. She simply identified, with stars on a map, the points she would like to see connected—Main Street, the elementary school road that also connects to the high school, and the like. Early on, she promised no land would be taken by eminent domain.

What she *did* do was ask each landowner to walk with her along the potential route:

> I had in my hand a map with stars, and told each landowner I was just looking for a way to connect those stars. I did not say—"Can I have your land?" Instead, I showed each owner a blank map with pencil marks that could be erased. The landowner was invited to draw, with a pencil, the way the path might go through their land. No one, I told each owner, knew their land as well as they did.
>
> What's more, I was grateful and contented with their worst land—along the edge of a cornfield, behind a dump, along the edge of river where we'd have to stabilize the rocks, sometimes a tree line "out back" that they never saw.

The operation was especially sensitive because a refusal *by any one owner* could have scotched the entire process and because a decision was made early on: No landowner could or would be paid cash for his or her land. If that had happened, each other person uncompensated might easily have felt that they had been taken.

What landowners were asked to sign was a deed of easement—a deed that Lusk, having gotten herself notarized, carried around with her to pick up instant signatures as agreements were obtained. (For the landowners, the density provisions of the Stowe zoning ordinance, allowing a specified number of units per acre, were a real concern. The agreement reached was that easements made for the recreation path would not be reduced from the total acreage reckoning used as a basis for a landowner's future development rights. In return, landowners received no town tax reductions for their recreation path land easements. For the town, there were no tax implications in these transactions—although a number of landowners subsequently obtained federal tax deductions for the value of their easements.)

The most effective point in getting landowners to grant easements, Lusk found, was the idea they were making a contribution of real value to their town—creating a path their children and their friends would come to enjoy:

> But it took lots of talking. I spent three months with one family farm, to get an easement. Three times a week, for three months running, I was out in their barn, wearing grubby jeans, just hanging out. They were the last people and also the biggest stretch of property. A deadline came up on which we'd lose a bundle of cash from the Federal Land Water and Conservation Fund if I didn't have all the easements completed. So I went to one brother in the barn, pleaded with him to sign. He said he would if his brother out at the woodpile would. I went to the brother at the woodpile and he agreed. So one signed, then the other.

Parallel to all this, Lusk had to work assiduously on the fund-raising front. The construction cost for the first phase of the path would be close to $300,000. Claire Lintilhac contributed $84,000—in a sense, a bittersweet story because she and her family firmly insisted the gift be anonymous; thus, Anne Lusk could never meet and personally share her enthusiasms and plans with the woman responsible for conceiving the path idea in the first instance.

Claire Lintilhac would die in the mid-1980s, between the completion of the first segment and planning for the second. While her own first vision had been for a safety pathway immediately beside the Mountain Road, her son Philip Lintilhac now agrees it was fortuitous that the path eventually took a less direct route, becoming "an integral part of the Stowe community" through its recreational uses. The scale and sharp turns of the route that was eventually selected, he noted, "discourage the high-speed bicycle racers who prefer the main road anyway." Town administrator Paul Hughes notes the idea of a pathway along the Mountain Road's shoulder proved impractical because the traffic is so heavy, driveways numerous, and snow plowed onto the shoulders during the winter.

The town was prevailed upon to make $42,000 in federal general revenue sharing money available for the project. A total of $118,000 was received in Land Water and Conservation Fund monies. Then there was the $53,000 that had to be raised in small local contributions—Lusk's toughest fiscal challenge. She solved it through such imaginative fund-raising techniques as "selling off" parts of the path. For a $2 contribution, one could buy an inch, for $15 a foot, for $45 a yard—and on up through rods, chains, and links to the largest private contributions. The contributors are now acknowledged in a plaque at the start of the path.

On the second segment of the path, completed later in the 1980s, the $380,000 total was shared among similar sources—$50,000 from the Lintilhac family, $20,000 from revenue sharing, $60,000 from the Federal Land Water and Conservation Fund, $130,000 in private contributions. By now, confidence in the project was growing so robustly that the town pitched in $120,000 of its own tax revenues.

All the while, Lusk was setting up support committees—of landowners, potential supporters, flower planters, indeed, support committees for any and all special purposes. The Stowe Rotary Club, an enthusiastic backer of the path from the start, cites numerous other local organizations that provided significant support, among them the Stowe public schools, the Stowe Winter Carnival Committee, the Stowe Cooperative Nursery, the Stowe Area Board of Realtors, and the Stowe Area Association, "which rightfully saw the major benefit the path could provide to the resort-based community."

How does Lusk believe she made it all work?

> First of all, there's the advance publicity, so that the minute you're ready to go out to your community, most of the critical questions have been raised—and answered.
>
> You have to make sure your own personality doesn't get in the way. For example, when I have joint meetings on the path, I will always have it in a comfortable home setting. Not set up chairs like a board of directors and audience. You need an informal roundtable feel.
>
> I craft the setting—constantly quote peoples' good ideas, and give them credit for their good ideas. The idea is to keep rewarding peoples' good ideas, encouraging the discussion.
>
> Especially when you're dealing with town officials, try not to give them a "yes" or "no" choice. Instead, go with three options—all of which you like. People like to have a choice. The minute they have a choice, they'll pick one of your alternatives. Then it becomes their idea.
>
> If there ever is a chance you'll be told "no," I tell them before the meeting ends that I'll be sending them more material.
>
> My technique is to come in talking dumb but with a full group of options. As you hear objections/problems, promise to go look for some solutions. The minute they get a tiny grain of their idea in there, the more they are for it. Every opportunity you can give to Selectmen, or other influential people to make suggestions, gives power to you. Is that manipulation? No, it's just how you work through human nature.
>
> You must be a facilitator, moderator, or shuttle diplomat. But you're not The Leader. You're a pied piper, or gentle ringmaster. You have to keep reminding yourself: the true leadership and ideas come from consensus.

Some people believe Lusk was *too* strong-handed and did not take enough time to form a sponsoring group as enthusiastic as she, but the broader sentiment seemed to be that Lusk, in fact, sought to share decisions and share credit with others whenever she could.

What everyone appears to agree on is that without her perseverance, her strength of personality, the Stowe Recreation Path might well never have come to pass.

Could Lusk have made the process a more "democratic" one, in which the townspeople themselves were more engaged in the design and execution of the path? Could the whole town have been "bought in" more to the entire planning process?

The question is not easily answered but Lusk, when we asked, offers this response:

> A committee might undertake this big a project. But then you have to delegate—one person who writes, one who fund-raises, one who designs, one who gets the deeds of easement. But you still need one name to receive the ideas, to have the mailing address. You need an individual to relate to, who really cares, who knows the whole issue—for example, Lady Bird Johnson with her passion for wildflowers along America's roads. People elsewhere can relate to Anne Lusk, with portable typewriter from high school, salary of $5,000 a year. So other people know it can be done quite simply. Committees don't inspire other people. People inspire other people. Sometimes the only thing I sell is enthusiasm.

The community leader who is tempted to play dictator on a project, Lusk notes, needs to understand that consensus is the one way to make his or her goal successful in the long run. Getting a project done is not a one-time thing. Unless there is a sense of ownership, of broad community participation, long-term maintenance of the project is sure to suffer.

## *A New Pathway, Step-by-Step*

Walking along the path site with landowners, letting them pencil in the route, was only one of multiple walks Anne Lusk had to make over the territory, again and again, before the Stowe Recreation Path could become a reality. There had to be a walk with an engineer to determine the feasibility of each piece of the route*; then with a tree surgeon, marking every tree to come out, every one to stay; next with the bulldozer operator, guiding him each step; then she marked the path's curves with spray paint, walking ahead of the grader to dissuade him from his usual straight lines.

A lot of the design work, Lusk recalls, had to be done solo—it

*The engineering, even of a recreation path, requires major attention. The engineer hired, William Kules of Stowe, was obliged to develop rather exact construction plans and acquire a whole range of necessary local, state, and federal permits. He then oversaw the construction phase and prepared an "as-built right-of-way plan" for recording easement acquisitions.

is tough to take a town of 3,200 inhabitants with you step-by-step through the woods, but whenever people were with her on the site, from bulldozer operator to engineer, she encouraged their participation. "Because," Lusk suggests, "there are a lot of judgment calls, at the moment, and aesthetics by consensus may have the broadest long-term appeal."

What effect was she trying to create? She replies:

> A rhythm and alteration of views. The path is intended to be slow-paced, to give people private rooms to walk through, to give them surprises—from practically no view to the most spectacular, from a beautiful Vermont farm to a dumpster. From shade to sun, dappled trees to farm field, brook to mountain. I think it's because people are reacting to a constantly changing setting, they also react to other people on the path.

Tree selection was critical—a mix of hemlocks and sugar maples for bright hues of fall leaves on the pathway, for example. The overhead canopy is "carved" to make sure blocks of sun hit the path:

> You have dappled sunlight. You have solid shade. You make people come blinking out of dark forest into the full sunlight. Then you tease them back into the woods. You surprise them with a shot of a stream. And you take their breath away with the view of mountain.

One of the most charming elements of the path is its closeness to the West Branch River—indeed, the path crosses the river ten times, the result of landowners' various wishes that at first had seemed a cost burden but in time has turned out, with the visual interest of the bridges, to add variety and interest to the walk. *Water* turns out to be one of the Stowe Recreation Path's most stunning assets. The town is legitimately enjoying the recovery of views and use of a river that for many decades had been ignored and relegated to farmers' and a few residents' backyards, oftentimes hidden behind layers of scrub growth, mostly on private property.

Through the river, the Stowe Recreation Path reintroduces the sounds and flashing light of water into peoples' daily lives. Water becomes company—a companion, even when one is alone on the path. The water is there to reflect moods of weather, provoking new human reactions as the seasons, light, the clouds shift. It reveals itself in an infinitely more immediate, delight-inspiring fashion for pathway walkers and bikers than motorists could ever expect to experience.

Lusk thinks it is important that town greenways *go* somewhere—that they do not simply peter out, as if the funding had suddenly run out. The Stowe Recreation Path, for its part, starts right

***"The path is intended to be slow-paced," says Anne Lusk, "to give people private rooms to walk through."*** *(Photograph courtesy of Jeff Turnau, Stowe, Vermont)*

in the middle of Stowe Village, close to picturesque broad fields and a stunning church steeple view, and it *does* go someplace—it ends up at Stowe's Brook Road, with the riverbed and a covered bridge at the end. A circle of benches, a parking lot, a group of picnic benches, and a view are the kinds of element one should seek for any path's end, Lusk suggests.

The "furniture" and amenities along Stowe's path—the benches, signs, parking areas, road intersections—have been fairly characterized as "austere." They are well placed, the benches for example commanding some of the premier views. Stunning views there are along this pathway—church steeples, a collection of splendid old barns, broad meadows where cows graze, groves of trees, the riverscape, and Mount Mansfield.

***The path crosses the West Branch River ten times. The water, once visible to only a few farmers and landowners, has become an asset shared by all.*** *(Photograph courtesy of Nancy Cohn, Stowe, Vermont)*

There is a certain austerity to the overall design; it reflects not just the Vermont parsimony but Lusk's aversion to anything save a fairly unostentatious "people's path" through the town. There is an unobtrusive sign on Main Street indicating the path's start. The Mountain Road itself offers peekaboo glimpses of the path—a deliberate effort to stimulate tourists' interest—but this path, insists Lusk, "is supposed to be casually found, like a surprise, a delightful sidewalk. We don't want to hawk it as if it were a waterslide or some other gimmicky tourist attraction."

Not that everything went according to plan. Originally, as town administrator Hughes recalled, a series of quite attractive, supposedly theft-proof signs were placed along the path, but "people took tools to the path to steal the signs. Plainer signs of painted plywood have been installed and not stolen."

The path seems to welcome peoples' own additions, and it is easy to sense growing town ownership of the path. Various groups of citizens, from kids to church groups, have planted beds of flowers along the path and maintain them. Lusk has even had people working with her on wildflower beds. All sorts of unplanned uses have evolved—for instance, places where kids have their tree houses or have discovered summertime watering holes ideal for a quick dip.

## *Where Else?*

Is the Stowe Recreation Path a special, very *unique* event in American city and town planning? In one sense, it is not. All sorts of other communities across the nation have—and are increasingly constructing—greenways and recreation paths connecting foot networks of one type or another.

The 1987 Report of the President's Commission on Americans Outdoors endorsed the concept: "We recommend communities establish greenways, corridors of private and public recreation land and waters, to provide people with access to open spaces close to where they live, and to link together the rural and urban spaces in the American landscape."

Little matter that the Reagan administration's Council on Environmental Quality subsequently expunged the word "greenway" from the final official report, the excuse being that greenways can be "mechanisms for land use planning, restricting growth or regulating development." With or without the political ideologues' approval, the movement is catching on. Across the nation, there are said to be some five hundred greenway projects in place or under way.

One of the most exciting is the Brooklyn/Queens Greenway, which by 1995 will link Brooklyn's great parks, running forty miles from the Atlantic Ocean to Long Island Sound. It could even be outshone by the Ridge Trail, a four hundred-mile loop around the greater San Francisco Bay Area, of which seventy-five miles have already been completed.

There is the modest 1976 Bicentennial path that threads its way from downtown Bartelsville, Oklahoma, through woods, across streams, over hill and dale, to a terminus at a beautiful Frank Lloyd Wright–designed park. There is the Platte River Greenway close by the center of Denver; and Portland, Oregon, has its forty-mile loop, actually a 140-mile system of protected hiking and bicycle trails that traverse the forested hills and corridors of the Columbia and Willamette. Scheduled for completion sometime in the 1990s, the forty-mile loop trail skirts wetlands, makes its way through ravines and along ridge tops, and overlooks vistas and natural areas. Planning is currently under way to extend this greenway trail system to the coast. The new "Greenway to the Pacific" will be a boom to human recreation as well as ensuring a protected pathway for wildlife.

Keith Hay, director of American Greenways in Arlington, Virginia, says the national push for greenways is "growing by leaps and bounds" and "is largely a citizens movement to make the places where we live and work more habitable and humane."

*Common Ground,* a newsletter published by the Conservation Fund, declares:

> Greenways are mysterious. They defy precise definition, but their very elusiveness confers magical qualities. Somehow they galvanize whole communities. The secret lies in their general characteristics: they're green; they go somewhere; they form boundaries. Something deep in our species is drawn to such properties. To borrow a famous legal dictum: we may not be able to define the concept, but we know it when we see it.
>
> The glory of the greenway rests, in fact, on its wonderful elasticity. Pull it this way, and it covers the natural contours of ridgelines and watercourses. Push it that way, and it incorporates the designed infrastructure of abandoned railroads and utility corridors. It fits the local context. Across the country, greenways are sprouting in astonishing diversity, each generating its own mix of costs, goals, leaders, timing, rationale, and scale.

Not surprisingly, with Stowe's path completed, Lusk began attending conferences, prevailing on George Bush's White House to declare the Stowe path one of his "thousand points of light," evangelizing for the pathway idea across the nation.

Yet it is important to note what specially sets the Stowe Recreation Path apart from its myriad sister projects across the nation. Stowe's uniqueness, one is led to conclude, lies not in its natural beauty or design (though it does well on both those fronts) nor is Stowe's uniqueness limited to the enhanced sociability mentioned earlier in this chapter. The special contribution, rather, is its striking success as a town organizing principle. Here is a simple pathway that has begun to reorganize peoples' lives, to wean them from overwhelming automobiled dependency, and to return them to a more human scale of settlement and living.

Anne Lusk recalls the movie *Picnic,* when backyards were not fenced; when youngsters skipped from one back screen door to another. She recalls the time when people socialized on the sidewalk and by visiting on front porches. She laments:

> Now with fenced-in backyards, private barbecues, dangerous roads, and recreation facilities and elementary schools so far removed from the center of town—to socialize you have to receive or make a phone call, get into a car, and drive to someone else's house. You've lost the spontaneous heartwarming sociability of a small town.

If a recreation path can be sited just right—connecting housing areas, schools, businesses, the main street, playing fields, and natural vistas—then, the Stowe example suggests, it can begin to reorganize peoples' lives. (Stowe even has a McDonald's right beside the path. The familiar arch sign is cut way down in size—no gaudiness in *this* town, of course—but what the McDonald's means is that kids, and many adults, can spend a full day on the path, stopping by for a snack when they need it.)

Provide a pathway, the Stowe experience shows, and in a society where it seems people scarcely exist if they do not have an automobile, the pedestrian and bike rider can again claim equal status. Stowe is finding that people drive to the recreation path, bikes mounted on their vehicles, and then drop off children to bike there for hours. Seniors often motor to the path so they can enjoy it.

What all this suggests is that a pathway has the potential of changing peoples' preferred place of residence—from outlying, essentially isolated locations to housing closer to the town center, surely closer to the recreation path. Is it too much to hope that strategically placed pathways could cut back on the "suburbanization" of America's smaller towns and cities, the phenomenon of people moving to locations farther and farther out of town centers, by their personal decisions inflicting great harm on the traditional town centers? Could pathways make towns more lively and help to save the roads between towns from creeping development that fills up and mars, like billboards, the natural landscape?

Only time will tell—the experience not just of a Stowe, with its strong planning ethic and its heavy pull of outside dollars, but the experience of more normal towns.

Are recreation paths appropriate for just "plain old places"? Lusk is convinced they are, and that the argument to get less affluent places to try paths is not to talk about jogging or lovely views or getting people close to flora and fauna but rather:

> I would sell a path strictly as a safe route for their kids to get around town when mom and dad are working. Because both parents have to work in the summertime and kids can't get to the swimming hole or a friend's house because they have to be driven. Build a path and all children, all ages have a safe way to get around town, all year long. And it's as good as providing after-school and weekend activities.
>
> And you don't have to do it all at once. In a town without a lot of money, it's OK to create just a dirt path. Use town equipment to remove topsoil, put down gravel from town supplies, and in ten years get to paving it. But get the permanent right of way. It's critical to have the path in the right location, and to have acquired the land.

In Stowe, Vermont, the path seems truly to have changed lives, especially for younger people. Suddenly, they are freed from excessive dependence on those adult chauffeurs we often refer to as parents. Gone are the days of being isolated at home or riding one's bike in circles around the elementary school parking lot because it is too dangerous to venture out on the street. Now kids can go independently to hang out with their friends. They gang together on the path, boasts Lusk, "like swarms of bees." There have even been whole birthday parties on the path, with mothers bringing cakes and the kids their swimsuits for a dash to one of the watering holes on the river.

Is the model applicable in city neighborhoods, in urban areas where there is so much more fear of crime? The answer has to depend, of course, on the locality, on the path's route, on the interest and commitment of neighbors. One has to believe that if urban neighborhood paths are oriented, more and more, to connecting the vital areas—from stores to homes to schools to playgrounds—then their chances of success in rebuilding American community, creating a new common ground, will inevitably escalate.

***The path offers a change from the car culture. Providing kids independence and safety, it can free parents from the relentless role of chauffeur.*** *(Photograph courtesy of Jeff Turnau, Stowe, Vermont)*

## *Commentary: Stowe*

ANNE WHISTON SPIRN: If the idea of the Rudy Bruner Award is to present models of success for others to learn from, then the Anne Lusk model is a very important one for community leaders to think about. We recently completed a report in Philadelphia, *Models of Success: Landscape Improvement and Community Development,* where we looked at necessary components for success in projects like this. One is clearly the key individual, but to sustain a project, that individual must be able to share success with others. We found that a person who cannot work with others may be able to initiate a project but the success will be limited.

ROBERT SHIBLEY: I think it is a troublesome model. Lusk's negotiations were one-on-one: property owner with Anne. Nowhere did the pressure of several property owners sitting together in a room come to grips with the notion that "If you'd give up this much more, the path would be this much better." Community action should be held in a forum where community consensus can be achieved. Because that didn't happen, the idea of this place is very much more beautiful than the reality of it.

SPIRN: The process may not have been ideal, but no one came in and said, "You must put the path here; we are taking this land by eminent domain."

SHIBLEY: But if property owners feel that they gave their land grudgingly—as opposed to feeling that they had made the first of a number of significant contributions to the quality of a shared environment—then the path will reflect that difference over time.

SPIRN: Megaprojects funded by a single source make it hard for individuals to see their own mark. Stowe was funded an inch at a time. Instead of hiring one landscape architect and someone to build, small groups had the opportunity to create small landscapes. Girl Scouts made a wildflower meadow. A lot of people feel ownership.

It was a monumental accomplishment, and it allowed Stowe to meet one of our other criteria critical for success: permanent ownership and control of the land. Many landscape improvement projects are done on land to which people have only temporary access. That makes the project vulnerable. Without that sense of ownership, you lose what you have at Stowe: kids building tree houses or having birthday parties there.

But our report notes that good design is also a critical part of success.

**SHIBLEY:** There is no design in this path other than the somewhat serendipitous decisions made by Lusk walking around with landowners. The only vision was: There should be a path and it should be on the least valuable land, the land most likely to be donated. That's not a vision that necessarily creates a wonderful community backyard or reverses the front yard/backyard dynamic of a community. Stowe sends the message that the easiest way is okay instead of seeking the best way. That's not to deny that thirty-two separate land deals and sixty signatures were required to put this thing together. It was an act of will.

In this case, unfortunately, the process was the design. A better alternative is to recognize a set of technical and aesthetic understandings about, say, how a bridgehead meets the land on both sides or where flowers might be positioned to define a place for a bench. A bench and a wastebasket don't establish the definition of a place.

**SPIRN:** The path works as well as it does because it uses two extremely powerful archetypal features: One is water and the other is path. Think about the great social spaces, the boulevards of Paris, even Sunset Strip. These are places to see and be seen. They are movement, boundary, rendezvous, places to go without committing yourself socially. The ten bridges were originally seen as unfortunate because they increased the cost, but bridges are also an archetype. They pass over. They give you views from the center of the stream. They punctuate the path and provide a place to meet.

Anne Lusk is not a designer, but in her sequential description of the path, where she explains how one emerges from dark to light, from close-in views of flowers to broad views of mountains, she is articulating very good design principles. A path is more interesting if it's not all obvious. You know you're going somewhere but you get surprises along the way.

**SHIBLEY:** I don't believe the people of Stowe perceive this as their path. I think they perceive it as Anne's path. Will the flower gardens be maintained? Will people embellish and improve the path? Does everyone whose property backs onto the path feel the obligation to turn the place where the garbage cans are stored into something different? Is there a commitment to the place?

I think the answer is no. When I visited, the backs of buildings were not being remade to address the public thoroughfare to which they were now exposed. You see the garbage and the parking lots. There isn't continuing pressure to improve the backs of buildings because the social infrastructure is not in place. Of course, improvements may still emerge.

**SPIRN:** The rough spots gradually can be transformed over time as people recognize that some parts of the path are more beautiful than others. Every project doesn't have to be "high design," though I am a fan of high design. If it's working, and transforming the way people meet each other, if it's giving children the experience of transforming their own community by their own actions, then that is an aesthetic of its own. The path can be appreciated as vernacular design.

Another factor contributing to the success of projects is having clearly defined goals. In Stowe, one stated goal was that the kids should get a safe place to ride their bikes. With goals like this clearly stated at the outset, you are in a position to look back and say, "Yes, we did it." And in Stowe, they did.

# Index